SEX EDUCATION

A Young Person's Guide

Charlotte Crowder

Sex Education – A Young Person's Guide is also available in accessible formats for people with any degree of visual impairment. The large print edition and eBook (with accessibility features enabled) are available from Need2Know. Please let us know if there are any special features you require and we will do our best to accommodate your needs.

First published in Great Britain in 2012 by
Need2Know
Remus House
Coltsfoot Drive
Peterborough
PE2 9BF

Telephone 01733 898103
Fax 01733 313524
www.need2knowbooks.co.uk
SB ISBN 978-1-86144-242-0
Cover photograph: Dreamstime

Contents

Introduction

Right now, you may be eager for all sorts of new experiences. Or, you may feel things are happening a little too fast. As a pre–teen or teen, you may be making some of your own choices for the first time.

Some of your hardest choices will have to do with your sexuality. Today, sexual standards are confusing. Most of your life, you've been blasted with mixed messages about sex. Messages from TV, movies, the Internet, music and adverts. Now's the time to make up your own mind. First, get the facts you need to make the right choices for yourself.

This book aims to give you good information. It starts with the facts. Some of these you may already know. You can skip to the sections you most want to learn about, by checking the Contents guide.

The second part is to help you think about choices you will face. Weigh the information against your personal values. Above all, take time to learn about yourself and the people you feel closest to. Make positive choices now to safeguard your health and happiness for the future.

There's lots of slang for body parts and sex acts. These terms are not always respectful. And often different groups of people use different slang. For these reasons, this book uses formal terms.

Medical and scientific words that might be new to you are explained in the book chapters. These words are also listed with their meanings in a glossary. If you want to be reminded of the meanings, check the glossary on page 95.

Lots of medical words are based on Greek or Latin words. So, you may also learn a little Greek and Latin when you read this book.

You can read this book alone or together with an adult. If you have questions or concerns about anything you read here, ask an adult. It should be someone with whom you feel comforTable discussing these topics. It could be a parent, teacher, counsellor, or health-care provider. You might be surprised how much information they have to share.

At the end of the book there is a help list. It includes websites and agencies that can provide more information or helpful advice. There are also books suggested for further reading. You can share the help list with the adults you may include in talks on these topics.

Disclaimer

This book provides general information about sexual health and personal safety. Information about alcohol, drugs and the Internet is intended to promote safe use within legal guidelines.

Every effort had been made to give valid information. It is considered up-to-date as of the book's print date. None of this information should replace professional medical advice. For questions about your own sexual or emotional health or contraception needs, ask a health-care provider or clinic.

Part One

Just the Facts

'Knowledge is power'.

Francis Bacon

This section presents the basic facts about sexuality.
Take power over your future. Know the facts.

Chapter One
Changes

Puberty – What it is and when it happens

Puberty is when your body changes from a child's to an adult's. It's a slow process. It usually takes about two or three years.

It happens at a different time for everyone. The timing is probably different for you and for your classmates.

For girls, changes can start between about ages nine and 14. But earlier or later is normal too. For boys, changes can start between about ages 11 and 15. Again, earlier or later is also normal.

Find out when these changes happened for your relatives. Chances are the timing will be similar for you.

'The word "puberty" comes from the Latin word for "adult".'

Hormones – What they are and how they work

Hormones are your body's natural chemical messengers. Your glands produce hormones. Your body has many different glands. Each gland produces different kinds of hormones. The hormones travel through your bloodstream and signal your body to change.

The 'master' gland

The pituitary gland is often called the 'master' gland. The pituitary gland is in your brain. It's just behind the bridge of your nose. It's only about the size of a pea, yet it's in charge of all your other glands. It produces lots of different hormones.

One hormone the pituitary produces is growth hormone. That controls how fast and tall you grow. During puberty the pituitary sends out extra growth hormone. You may grow very fast.

The pituitary also signals your body's maturing. It produces special hormones to do this. From your brain, it sends hormone signals to your sex glands to start making their own special hormones.

Fertility

All creatures from the tiniest insect to the largest animal are designed to reproduce – to make more of their own kind. The sex organs of the human body are designed to reproduce.

You are born with your sex organs in place. But during puberty they change and grow.

The changes of puberty make you fertile. From then on you are capable of having children.

The important parts – sex organs

Here we'll start with the terms for sex organs, also called genitals. There are pictures. That way, you can see what they look like. Later, we'll talk in more detail about how all these parts work.

Female parts

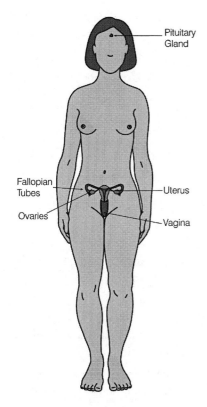

Fig.1 Girl's Body

Labels on figure:
- Pituitary Gland
- Fallopian Tubes
- Ovaries
- Uterus
- Vagina

What's inside?

Girls have a uterus inside the lower part of their belly. It is about the shape and size of an upside-down pear. It can stretch to hold a growing baby. In the picture on page 12 you can see there are two fallopian tubes. One is on each side of the uterus. At the end of each fallopian tube is an ovary. Each ovary is about the size of a peach stone. The ovaries contain eggs, called ova. Each single ovum is about the size of the full stop at the end of this sentence.

At the bottom of the uterus, where the pear's stem would be, is the cervix. The cervix is the inside opening to the uterus. The cervix connects to the vagina. The vagina is the opening to the outside of the woman's body. The vagina is amazingly stretchy.

'Ovum is Latin for "egg". Ova is the plural of ovum.'

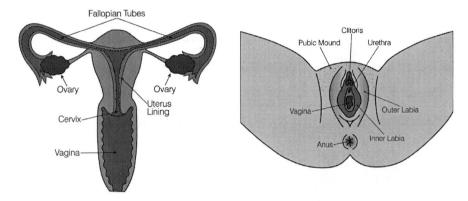

Fig.2 What's Inside a Girl's Body

Fig.3 The Vulva

What's outside?

What's outside is called the vulva. The word vulva comes from the Latin word for 'covering'. That's what it does. It covers the opening to the vagina. The vulva is made up of:

- Labia – Soft flesh on each side of the opening to the vagina. The word labia comes from the Latin word for 'lips'. And the labia do look like lips. There are two sets: the outer labia and inside them, the inner labia.

- The clitoris – Tucked at the top of the outer labia. What you see looks like a fleshy little button or a very tiny finger. Behind that is a complex system of nerves.

- The pubic mound – Pillow-like flesh that covers the pubic bone.

The vulva also covers the opening of the urethra, where it carries urine out of the body. The urethra is in front of the opening to the vagina.

Just behind the vulva is the anus. The anus is the outside opening of the rectum. The rectum is the end portion of the bowels.

Male parts

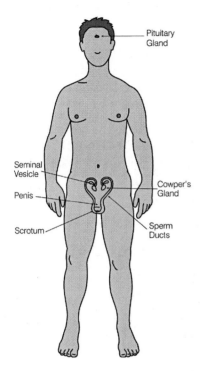

Fig.4 Boy's Body

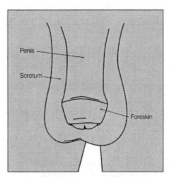

Fig.5 Uncircumcised Penis

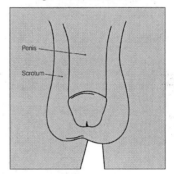

Fig.6 Circumcised Penis

What's outside?

All boys are born with a hood of skin that covers the head of the penis. It's called the foreskin. Boys who are uncircumcised still have their foreskins. If boys are circumcised, the foreskin is removed. Circumcision is usually done when a boy is an infant. Sometimes circumcision is part of a religious ceremony.

Boys have two testicles. Each testicle is about the size of a walnut. A pouch of skin, called the scrotum, holds the testicles. A boy's anus is just behind the testicles.

What you don't see

The testicles make sperm. Sperm are microscopic in size. You can't see them with your naked eye. In the testicles, they start out immature.

Inside the testicles and the lower belly is a complex system of tubes:

▓ The urethra – A tube that runs from the bladder and the length of the penis. It serves a double purpose. It carries urine out of the body. During sex it carries semen out. The system works so urine and semen never mix.

▓ The epididymis – Long tubes that coil behind the testicles. The epididymis acts like a storage tank. It holds the sperm that the testicles make. It's here that the sperm mature. Then each one is capable of fertilising an ovum and starting a pregnancy.

▓ The sperm ducts – Tubes that carry sperm to the urethra.

Other parts add fluids to the sperm to make semen.

▓ Seminal vesicles – Attached to the sperm ducts below the bladder.

▓ The prostate – Bridges the urethra.

▓ Cowper's glands – Below the prostate, on the sides of the urethra.

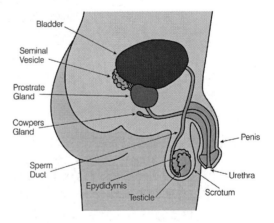

Fig.7 What's Inside a Boy's Body

The skin of the penis is loose and stretchy. Inside the skin is soft spongy tissue. And like a sponge, it has lots of little spaces. There are actually thousands of spaces. With sexual excitement, blood flows into the spaces. The extra blood flow to all those spaces makes the penis erect, it stands up straight. The liquid semen then transports the sperm through the system of tubes. When the semen comes out of the urethra, it's called ejaculation.

Sex hormones

For a girl, the ovaries are the main sex glands. When they get the signal from the pituitary, the ovaries start making special hormones. These are called oestrogen and progesterone.

For a boy, the main sex glands are testicles. The testicles make their own special hormone when they get the pituitary's signal. It's called testosterone.

Sex hormones travel from your sex glands through your body. They slowly start the changes of puberty.

Girls' body changes

If you are a girl, the first changes you notice may be in your nipples. Slowly, over weeks or months, your nipples will start to swell. Sometimes, one nipple swells first. This is normal. One or both may feel sore.

Then, slowly your breasts will grow. It takes about three years for them to grow to their full size. Again, one breast may grow faster than the other. This too is normal. They will even out in the end.

How large or small your breasts are depends on your genes. Your genes determine most of your physical traits. If your mother and your aunts have full breasts, chances are you will too. If they have smaller breasts, you probably will.

The size of your breasts is not a measure of sexiness. Small is beautiful too.

While your breasts are growing, you will probably grow taller. Your shape will begin to change too. Your hips and thighs will get rounder. You will get a more distinct waist.

'For a girl, the ovaries are the main sex glands. For a boy, the main sex glands are testicles.'

Fine hairs will start to grow between your legs. Over time, they will grow thick and curly. They will form a triangle on your lower belly. You'll grow hair under your arms too.

Your vulva starts out flat and smooth. As you mature, it will darken. Your outer labia will grow to small mounds. Your inner labia will get looser and a bit wrinkled. Your clitoris will grow too.

How a girl becomes fertile – What's going on inside

You are born with a lifetime's supply of ova in your ovaries. About two or three years after your breasts start to grow, your female sex hormones will signal your ova to ripen. From then on you are fertile. That means you are capable of becoming pregnant and having a baby.

Ova ripen one tiny ovum at a time. One ripens each month. As an ovum ripens, the ovary lets it go. The ovaries take turns at this. So, every other month each ovary lets one ovum go.

The ovum travels down one of the fallopian tubes. The ovum's trip from the ovary down the tube to the uterus is called ovulation. This is the time when you are fertile. The trip takes several days.

During the ovum's trip, your sex hormones signal your uterus to prepare for the possibility of pregnancy. Your uterus builds a rich lining of blood to nurture a pregnancy. At the end of the fallopian tube, the ovum reaches your uterus.

The ovum dissolves if it is not fertilised by a sperm. Changing hormone signals let the uterus know there is no pregnancy. The uterus then sheds the unneeded lining. The lining leaves your uterus through your vagina. This is called the menstrual flow. The flow is not like blood from an injury. It may be red, but is often brownish. It can be thick or somewhat lumpy. The flow usually lasts about three days to a week. That's how long it takes your uterus to shed the lining.

The whole cycle from when an ovum begins to ripen to when it dissolves generally lasts a period of about a month. That's why the menstrual flow is often called a 'period'. When you first start to have periods, your cycles will

'The whole cycle from when an ovum begins to ripen to when it dissolves generally lasts a period of about a month. That's why the menstrual flow is often called a "period".'

probably be quite irregular. There may be several months between your periods, or they may come more often. This irregularity is normal. It's because your hormones' signals aren't yet fully mature.

A few notes about periods

Many girls and women feel more emotional before or when they are having their periods. This is a normal result of hormone surges at this time in monthly cycle.

Your period should not keep you from your usual activities. And you should feel well.

The uterus contracts as it sheds its lining. This is the reason some girls have cramps. Cramps can be in your belly or lower back. If you do have cramps, usually a mild pain medicine will relieve them. Ask your mother, your health-care provider or another adult to recommend what pain medicine to take.

At first you will probably use pads during your periods. The pads fit in your underwear to catch the flow. You'll need to change them every few hours. How often depends on how heavy your flow is.

Once you get comforTable with the process, you may want to use tampons. Tampons are made of absorbent material. They fit inside your vagina to soak up your flow. Many come with applicators to insert them. Before you use a tampon for the first time, ask for advice. Ask someone who knows how to insert it. It should be someone you are comforTable talking to about this.

The size tampon you use and how often you change tampons will depend on your flow. You may use super-sized tampons when your flow is the heaviest. Later in your period, you may use a smaller size. Your vagina stretches to whichever size you use. It will hold a tampon securely. A tampon can't fall out.

- Use the smallest size tampon possible for each day's flow.
- Never use more than one tampon at a time.
- Change tampons every four to six hours during the day.
- Change tampons first thing in the morning.
- Only use a tampon when you have your period.

If you ever need to change a pad or tampon more often than once an hour, tell an adult right away. This may be a sign something is wrong. Seek advice from your health-care provider, such as your GP.

Boys' body changes

If you are a boy, the first change you'll likely notice is that your testicles get bigger. They will probably double in size. Most boys have one testicle that hangs lower.

Your scrotum will grow to hold your testicles. The skin of your scrotum will darken. The tiny bumps on your scrotum are where hairs will begin to grow.

Next, your penis will start to get wider and longer.

Penises and testicles come in all sizes. Size has nothing to do with sexual abilities. And most girls don't care much about size.

'Penises and testicles come in all sizes. Size has nothing to do with sexual abilities.'

Pubic hair will grow on your lower belly and between your legs. Over about three years it gets thicker and curlier. Then hair will also grow under your arms.

You'll likely have a growth spurt. You'll grow taller. You'll probably get more muscular. Your shape will change. Your shoulders will get wider.

After your growth spurt, your voice changes. That's because your voice box and vocal cords are getting bigger. As your voice deepens, it may sometimes 'crack'. Suddenly, in the middle of a sentence, it might get high and squeaky. This can be embarrassing. But it's very normal.

Another embarrassment can be changes in your chest. Your nipples may be sore. They may actually enlarge somewhat. Some boys even get a bit of fat behind their nipples. Don't worry. This goes away. It's due to changes in hormones.

Your facial hair starts to grow about two years after your pubic hair appears. Hair starts to grow on your legs and arms around that time. Chest hair comes later.

How a boy becomes fertile

Most boys have erections even as babies. From the first time you ejaculate semen, you are fertile. All those tubes work now. That means you are capable of making a girl pregnant and becoming a father.

You'll likely have wet dreams and ejaculate during your sleep. This happens to all boys during puberty. It's your body testing the new system.

Another way boys' bodies seem to test the system is with unexpected erections. They can appear for no reason at all. Usually out of any sexual context. These are normal too. Knowing that doesn't make them easy to handle. They can be a source of serious embarrassment. Over time you will get fewer.

Body image

With all these changes going on, it might take time to get used to your new body. You will get comforTable with it. Remember, no one shape is better than another. There are all different body types.

Chances are your body changes at a different rate from your classmates'. You may be ahead or behind. Whichever, you will likely feel awkward. Everyone does.

Your body will need more food. Growth spurts can make you hungry all the time. You may need to eat a lot more than you used to. And more often.

Growth spurts can make you clumsy. It takes time for your muscle coordination to catch up with your growth. You may trip over your feet. Or you may drop things. You might feel gawky. Once the spurt is over, your muscles will coordinate with your limbs.

Even the way you smell will change. You'll want to think about using deodorant. You may sweat a lot more than you used to. Antiperspirants can help with this.

Sex hormones can make your skin and hair oily. Changes in your skin can lead to acne. There are many products for teen skin and hair care. Take a trip to the chemist. Check what's there. Try a few products. See what works best for you. If you have bad acne, talk to your health-care provider.

Brain changes – How your brain develops

All this and your brain is changing too.

One of the first areas of your brain to mature has to do with emotions. You will likely find it easier to talk about how you feel. You may also start to think more deeply. And your thoughts may be very different from your parents' thoughts.

Meanwhile, the area of your brain behind your forehead grows. This is like the control panel of your brain. Over your teen years, your reasoning and planning skills will change. But this doesn't happen all at once. That control panel isn't fully wired to the rest of your brain until adulthood. The pleasure-seeking part of your brain develops first. That might mean not all of your decisions will be good ones.

A child's brain has lots and lots of connections. That's because there is so much to learn about the world at first. Now, the structure of your brain changes. Many connections get trimmed away. You may leave many childhood interests behind and find you focus on just a few that are of serious interest.

At this time in your life, your brain is considered plastic. That means it's easy to develop new connections in your brain. You can pursue new skills, talent and knowledge. You'll learn them easily.

'One of the first areas of your brain to mature has to do with emotions. You will likely find it easier to talk about how you feel.'

More hormones

Hormones in the teen brain change too:

- Melatonin is a hormone that makes you sleepy. Your daily supply of melatonin is on a different schedule than in childhood. So, it takes longer for you to get tired at night. And you probably want to sleep later. Plan your schedule to be sure you get enough sleep. You need 8½ to 9½ hours each night.

- Dopamine does many things for you. One thing it does is make you happy and excited. Babies and children have a lot of dopamine. Adults have less. Your supply of dopamine starts to go down during your teen years. But the supply is uneven. You will also get bursts of lots of dopamine.

Emotions

You'll have lots of ups and downs. There are lots of reasons.

At first your supply of sex hormones and dopamine is uneven. This can make you moody. Low levels of dopamine can make you tired. They might cause you to lose interest in things, or make it hard to concentrate. Bursts of dopamine can make you high on life. They can also produce intense sexual feelings.

Your body is changing in so many ways. You may feel uncomforTable in your own skin.

At this time, it's probably really important for you to fit in with your friends. Yet, you and your classmates all mature at your own rate. Some already look like adults. Some don't. You may not all care about the same things. This makes everyone feel insecure. Know that you are not alone.

With new brain changes, your thoughts might be different from your parents'. You may question rules at home and at school. You may feel closer to friends than family. All this can cause tension at home.

Summing Up

- Hormones signal the changes of puberty. You grow and change shape. Your emotions swing from high to low. It may take time to get comforTable with your new self.

- You will likely mature at a different rate from your classmates.

- The changes of puberty make you fertile. From then on you are capable of having children.

- At this time in your life, your brain is changing too. You'll think more deeply. It's easy to develop new connections in your brain right now. You'll learn new things easily.

Chapter Two
Sex and How it Works

The sex urge

The sex urge is strong in all animals. It's a physical response to the basic instinct to reproduce. This is true for human beings too. All those parts we talked about in the last chapter have a specific purpose. Everything about our bodies, male or female, is designed to make pregnancy possible. But we all know that there is a lot more to sex. There's pleasure too. And, at least for humans, there is a lot of emotion involved. It's called lovemaking, because it's the ultimate expression of love. And most often, reproduction is not the aim. We'll talk about all that later.

First, let's see how it all works.

Chemistry

First, there's attraction. Two people are drawn to each other. Sometimes it's just physical at first. The attraction can be immediate. This can be magical – 'love at first sight'. Maybe a man's shoulder blades are particularly pleasing. Perhaps a woman's neck is long and looks extra soft. Or, the couple's eyes meet and there is a special sparkle.

Attraction can also build from a close relationship. Over time, two friends who care a lot about each other may discover a physical attraction.

Physical attraction, what some call 'chemistry', is sexually exciting. You feel it in your sexual parts. Or, sometimes just in the pit of your stomach.

'Everything about our bodies, male or female, is designed to make pregnancy possible.'

Emotions

Sex can happen without good emotion. But ideally, it should be a way to share strong, positive feelings with a partner. And those strong feelings actually cue the physical changes that make good sex happen.

Touch

We all know how good a hug feels. It makes you feel cared for. It makes you feel close to the other person. It helps you relax.

Hugs, kisses and touch are important parts of what's called foreplay. Foreplay is a time of physically close sharing between partners. Foreplay can lead to more. Or, it can be enjoyed for the play itself. Couples can indulge in hours of such play. In the movies, foreplay never lasts long. But that is not reality.

Every square inch of your skin has more than one thousand nerve endings. What's more, skin becomes more sensitive to touch during foreplay. Breasts and nipples get more sensitive too. And it's not just the woman's nipples that are extra sensitive. A man's nipples react more also. All this probably explains a couple's urge to be naked together. All those extra sensitive nerve endings in the skin are yearning to be touched.

The touch of foreplay also cues physical changes.

Sexual excitement

All this hugging, kissing and touching results from sexual excitement. And it leads to more sexual excitement. That starts things happening.

This is where that system of tubes and fluids comes in. (See under 'Male parts', page 13.) The sperm the testicles made are in the epididymis. That's the storage tank we talked about. The sperm have matured here. Each one is now capable of starting a pregnancy.

Now the other parts get busy making semen. The seminal vesicles make a sugary fluid. The fluid works like an energy drink. It gives the sperm power to move. The prostate adds another fluid to give the sperm energy.

You'll remember that the male urethra has a double purpose. It carries urine and semen out of the body. But never at the same time. The Cowper's glands make a slippery fluid. The fluid neutralises any acid in the urethra before the semen travels through it.

The whole package, penis, testicles and scrotum, are all very sensitive to touch. That includes the parts of the penis behind the testicles. The penis has about 8,000 nerve endings. The clitoris, a woman's main pleasure center, has even more. But they are packed into that tiny button and the flesh behind it. With all those nerve endings, the clitoris is extremely sensitive.

We all have a special kind of skin. The most dramatic change of sexual excitement is to that skin. It has the unromantic name of erectile tissue. That just means it's skin that can stand up. It's the spongy tissue with spaces where blood flows during sexual excitement. (See again under 'Male parts', page 13.)

It's erectile tissue that makes a man's penis stand straight up. Women have erectile tissue too. A woman's clitoris has the same spongy tissue. And the inner labia of her vulva do too. With sexual excitement, her labia swell. And the head of her clitoris stands up.

With all that extra blood flow, a man's penis and a woman's vulva get bright and red. Things start to get slippery. With sexual excitement, the woman's vagina gets moist. Often the man's erect penis drips a tiny amount of semen. Even these tiny drops have sperm capable of starting a pregnancy. In vaginal intercourse a man's penis meets up with a woman's vagina. All this moisture makes it possible for the man to slide his erect penis into the woman's vagina. Her vagina stretches to hold his penis.

'Self pleasure is still another form of sexual expression. It's when a person explores his or her body alone.'

Other forms of sexual expression

Vaginal intercourse is not the only form of sexual expression. And sexual expression is not limited to couples of the opposite sex. Same-sex and opposite sex couples delight in each other's body parts. They may nibble ear lobes or suck on toes. In oral sex they explore each other's genitals with their mouths. Anal sex involves exploration of or intercourse with the anus and rectum.

Self-pleasure is still another form of sexual expression. It's when a person explores his or her body alone.

A special feeling

Sexual release often brings orgasm. Not everyone has orgasms all the time. And everyone experiences orgasm differently. It can be an all-over good feeling. It can be an intense feeling in the genitals. Or it can be a feeling somewhere in-between.

Orgasms can result from self-pleasure, a partner's special touch, or intercourse. For a man, orgasm usually results in the ejaculation of semen. Although a woman may not be as aware of it, her vagina also releases fluids during orgasm.

In the movies, it seems couples always have simultaneous orgasms. That is, both partners have an orgasm at exactly the same time. It doesn't happen that way all the time. Sometimes each partner has an orgasm at different times. Sometimes one partner does and the other doesn't. It's also possible for one or both partners to have multiple orgasms.

Orgasms can certainly add to a feeling of closeness between partners. But it is just as possible to feel close without orgasms.

The travels of a sperm and an ovum

In vaginal intercourse between a man and a woman, the friction of the man's penis against the inside of the woman's vagina can cause his orgasm. He releases about 400 million sperm in his semen.

The sperm swim toward the woman's cervix. When the woman is ovulating, the cervix is open to the uterus. When she is not ovulating, mucus blocks the sperm's entrance.

If the sperm make it past the cervix, they swim up through the woman's uterus. Then they swim up the fallopian tubes.

If the woman is ovulating, an ovum is coming down one fallopian tube. Or it is just getting ready to take the trip down. Sperm can live for several days. They can hang around until the ovum shows up in the fallopian tube. It takes just one sperm out of those 400 million to meet up with that ovum. When a single sperm comes together with an ovum, the ovum is fertilised. The fertilised ovum then seals itself off. That way no other sperm can enter the ovum. Then the unneeded sperm die off.

The fertilised ovum then continues down the fallopian tube. About three days later, it arrives in the uterus. There it spends another few days floating free.

Pregnancy

Four or five days after fertilisation, the fertilised ovum separates into two parts. One part will grow into an embryo. The other part will become the placenta. The placenta serves as the life support center throughout the pregnancy.

At the fertile time in a woman's monthly cycle, the uterus has built the rich lining of blood. The lining is there to nurture a pregnancy. About six to 12 days after fertilisation, the fertilised ovum settles into the lining of the uterus. The placenta attaches to the lining. As it does so, the placenta makes a pregnancy hormone. This is known as hCG. Some women have nausea early in pregnancy. If so, hCG is the cause.

In usual amounts, the female hormones, oestrogen and progesterone, control a woman's monthly cycle. But hCG signals the woman's body to make extra progesterone and oestrogen. The growing embryo needs the lining for nourishment. The extra progesterone makes sure the lining is not shed and the woman has no period. Often the first way a woman knows she might be pregnant is if her period does not happen. Enlarged and sore breasts can be another early hint of pregnancy caused by progesterone. The soreness is usually greater than what might happen before a period.

Pregnancy testing

hCG is what is measured by a pregnancy test. A pregnancy test can detect hCG in a woman's urine about one week after a missed period. For accurate results, usually the test must be done on the morning's first urine. Home tests are available at the chemist. Results are immediate. Each test has detailed instructions on the box.

There are also blood tests for hCG. These can be done even sooner than one week after a missed period. They must be done at a doctor's office or a clinic. It may take a few days to get results.

'hCG stands for human chorionic gonadotropin. The chorion is the outside covering of the embryo. A gonadtropin is a hormone that sends signals to sex organs.'

Trimesters

Pregnancy is divided into trimesters. These are dated from a woman's last monthly period. This is because the date of fertilisation is often hard to guess. The first trimester lasts to 12 weeks after the last monthly period.

First trimester

The placenta grows a network of blood vessels. These blood vessels connect the woman to the embryo. Nourishment from the woman's blood travels to the embryo's blood. Waste from the embryo's blood travels back to the woman's blood.

Around two weeks after fertilisation, the amniotic sac forms from the placenta. The amniotic sac encases the embryo. It fills with fluid. The fluid cushions the embryo, protecting it.

Later, the umbilical cord forms from the placenta. This happens around the fifth week of the embryo's development. The umbilical cord protects the blood vessels between the woman and embryo. It carries oxygen from the woman to the embryo.

Oestrogen keeps the placenta working well. Most important, it signals the growth of all the major organs in an embryo. By the end of about eight weeks all major systems have formed. Then it is no longer an embryo. From then until birth, it is called a foetus.

Second trimester

The second trimester lasts from week 13 to 27. By week 13, the placenta makes its own supply of oestrogen and progesterone. From then on, the placenta's supply of hormones controls the pregnancy. It also signals a woman's breasts to grow to prepare for breastfeeding an infant. By this time, the amniotic sac contains proteins and many other nutrients. These help the foetus grow. As the foetus grows, a woman's pregnancy begins to show.

Third trimester

The third trimester lasts from week 28 to 40, or birth. By week 37, the foetus is called full term. A baby born at 37 weeks has organs that work on their own.

Birth

Before a woman goes into labour, her cervix begins to soften. The opening widens to make room for the baby to be born. When a woman goes into labour, the amniotic sac usually breaks. The amniotic fluid flows out. In a normal vaginal birth, the baby comes down the vagina head first. The vagina stretches for the delivery.

Summing Up

- Everything about our bodies, male or female, is designed to make pregnancy possible. But there is a lot more to sex.

- Sex is called lovemaking, because it's the ultimate expression of love.

- There are many different forms of sexual expression.

- The lining of a woman's uterus nurtures a pregnancy.

- hCG is known as the 'pregnancy hormone'. The placenta makes hCG. hCG signals the changes of pregnancy. A pregnancy test can detect hCG in a woman's urine or blood shortly after a missed period.

Chapter Three

Contraception and How it Works

Contraception

Contraception is used to prevent pregnancy from happening. To work, contraception must be used every time a man and woman have sex. A single ovum doesn't stand a chance against 400 million sperm.

There are many types of contraception:

- Barrier methods prevent sperm from meeting an ovum.

- Spermicides kill sperm.

- Hormonal methods use chemicals that act like natural hormones to prevent pregnancy.

- Intrauterine devices – IUDs for short – hamper how sperm move. They prevent the sperm from reaching an ovum. They may also prevent a fertilised egg from implanting in the uterus.

- Natural family planning calculates the infertile days in a woman's monthly cycle. She and her partner must then agree to have sex only on those days that it is not possible for her to get pregnant.

Abstinence – not having sex at all – also prevents pregnancy.

This chapter has general information about contraception. There is more information in chapter 9. Table 1 on page 108 has a summary of all methods and provides some further details.

'To work, contraception must be used every time a man and woman have sex.'

Barrier methods

Barrier methods block the man's sperm from entering the woman's uterus. But the barrier may not be perfect. Sometimes it may rip or leak. To prevent pregnancy, it works best to use a barrier method together with a spermicide.

Barrier methods include:

- Male and female condoms.
- Diaphragms and cervical caps.

Male condom

The male condom is a tube the size and shape of a penis. The condom fits over the man's penis and traps sperm. That way, sperm can't reach the woman's uterus.

Female condom

The female condom is a small pouch, open at one end. It has rings at one or both ends. The female condom fits inside a woman's vagina. One ring holds it in place against her cervix. The open end of the pouch covers her labia. The condom blocks the man's sperm from reaching her uterus.

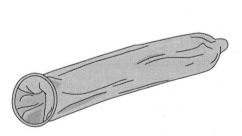

Fig.8 Male Condom

Fig.9 Female Condom

Diaphragm

The diaphragm is a dome with a flexible rim around the bottom. It is about as wide as the rim of a teacup, but not as deep. The diaphragm fits inside a woman's vagina. It covers the woman's cervix to block the man's sperm from reaching her uterus. The flexible rim holds the diaphragm in place and keeps sperm from leaking around the edges.

Cervical cap

The cervical cap looks like a large thimble. The cervical cap fits over a woman's cervix. Suction keeps the cap on her cervix. The cap blocks the man's sperm from reaching her uterus.

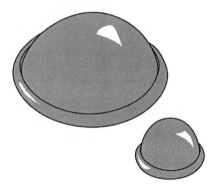

Fig.10 Diaphragm and Cervical Cap

Spermicides

Spermicides come in the following forms:

- Gel or cream.
- Foam.
- Vaginal contraceptive film – VCF.
- Suppositories.

Some male condoms are pretreated with spermicide.

Spermicides work best to prevent pregnancy when used together with a barrier method.

All forms come with an applicator. Using the applicator, a woman can insert the spermicide into her vagina before sex. She should do this if:

▪ She and her partner are using a spermicide alone.

▪ Her partner is using a male condom that is not pretreated with spermicide.

Spermicide gel or cream is used with diaphragms, cervical caps and female condoms. The woman should put the spermicide on the device first. Then she can insert the device in her vagina. With a diaphragm or cervical cap, the spermicide gel or cream goes inside the device. With a female condom, the spermicide goes on the outside of the closed end. This is the end that covers the cervix.

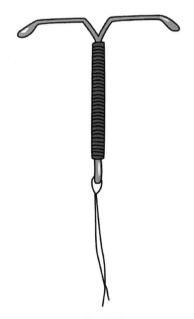

Fig.11 IUD

IUDs

An IUD fits inside a woman's uterus. It is about six centimetres long. It's T-shaped. It can be made of plastic or copper. A doctor or nurse inserts it through the opening of the cervix into a woman's uterus. The IUD can safely stay in the uterus for several years. A woman can get it removed if she wants to get pregnant.

Once in the uterus, the IUD changes the fluids in the uterus and the fallopian tubes. The changes hamper sperm's movement. The sperm can't reach the ovum. Fertilisation does not happen. The changes to the fluids may also prevent a fertilised egg from implanting in the uterus.

Hormone-based methods

Chemicals that act like the body's natural hormones can prevent pregnancy. Most hormone-based methods prevent ovulation. That way there is no ovum for a sperm to fertilise. The hormones also thicken the mucus in the opening of the cervix. This provides an extra safety back-up. The mucus prevents sperm from travelling into the uterus and into the fallopian tubes. Just in case there was an ovum making its way down the fallopian tube, no sperm could get there. All this makes it very unlikely an ovum could be fertilised. But if one were, the lining of the uterus could not nurture it. That's because the hormones thin the lining.

Hormone-based methods include:

- The pill.
- The patch.
- Contraceptive injections.
- Contraceptive implants.
- Vaginal ring.
- Intrauterine system – IUS for short.

Methods with oestrogen and progesterone

Combined contraceptive pills

A woman must take the pill on a regular schedule throughout each month. The schedule varies with different brands. It's very important to take the pill on schedule. There's a chance of pregnancy even with just one forgotten pill.

The patch

The patch is a sticking plaster. It releases the hormones through the skin. From the skin, the hormones get absorbed in the bloodstream. A woman wears one patch a week for three weeks. She skips the fourth week and wears no patch. The fourth week is the week of her period.

Vaginal ring

The vaginal ring is flexible plastic. It looks like a miniature bangle bracelet. It has an opening about five centimetres wide. A woman can insert the vaginal ring into her vagina herself. The exact position doesn't matter. She inserts it at the start of her period. It stays in place for three weeks. After that, the woman removes the ring herself. For continued contraception she inserts a new ring at her next period. While in place, the ring releases the hormones. The hormones get absorbed in the bloodstream.

Methods with progesterone only

Several methods contain only a form of progesterone – no oestrogen.

For the mini pill, the amount of progesterone alone is sometimes not enough to prevent ovulation. The mini pill works chiefly by thickening the mucus in the opening in the cervix. It blocks the sperm's entry.

For the following methods listed, the amount of progesterone is enough to prevent ovulation. It thickens the mucus in the opening of the cervix too. It also thins the lining of the uterus.

The mini pill

To avoid pregnancy, a woman must take the mini pill on a strict schedule at exactly the same time each day.

Contraceptive injections

A woman gets the injections once every eight or 12 weeks. How often depends on the brand. A doctor or nurse gives the injection into a muscle. Usually it's in the arm or buttocks.

Contraceptive implants

A contraceptive implant is about the size of a matchstick. It is flexible. A doctor or nurse inserts it under the skin of a woman's upper arm. It can stay there for up to three years to prevent pregnancy. It can be removed by a doctor or nurse at any time.

IUS

An IUS is much like an IUD. Like the IUD, a doctor or nurse inserts the IUS into a woman's uterus. The difference is that the IUS has a form of progesterone in it.

Natural family planning

Natural family planning calculates the infertile days in a woman's monthly cycle. She and her partner must then agree to have vaginal intercourse only on those days that it is not possible for her to get pregnant.

Abstinence

To abstain from, or not have, vaginal intercourse is like any other method of contraception. It has to be used every time. Otherwise, pregnancy is a risk.

Sterilisation

Sterilisation is a permanent form of contraception. It is surgery that is almost never possible to reverse. For that reason, it is only an option for people who:

- Have children and have definitely decided to have no more.
- Have definitely decided to have no children.

Sterilisation makes it impossible for ovum and sperm to meet. For a woman it seals off the fallopian tubes. Monthly hormones work as usual. The woman still has normal monthly periods. She still ovulates. But the ova can't get down her fallopian tubes. They are absorbed by her body. They can't reach her uterus. Fertilisation can't happen even if sperm are present.

For a man, sterilisation seals off the sperm ducts. This keeps sperm out of his semen. The sperm are absorbed by his body. He still ejaculates semen. Without sperm there can be no pregnancy.

'Emergency contraception is for when a contraceptive method fails or a couple has sex without contraception.'

Emergency contraception

Emergency contraception is for when a contraceptive method fails or a couple has sex without contraception.

Hormonal methods and how they work

Like regular contraception pills, emergency contraceptive pills have chemicals that act like natural hormones. They must be taken within just a few days after a single act of unprotected sex. (For more details, see chapter 9 and Table 1, page 108.)

If woman hasn't yet ovulated, the hormones delay ovulation. That way, they prevent fertilisation. Any sperm have died off before an ovum reaches the fallopian tube. At the same time, the hormones thin the lining of the uterus. If fertilisation has happened, the lining is not able to nurture the fertilised ovum.

Copper IUD insertion

A copper IUD can be inserted within five days of unprotected sex. As you've read, an IUD can hamper sperm's movement. This may prevent fertilisation in those first few days. It is also likely that the IUD changes the lining of the uterus. It takes six to 12 days before a fertilised ovum settles in the lining of the uterus. By that time, the lining thins and would no longer nurture the fertilised ovum.

More male contraception is the future

Up to now the only contraception men use is the condom. Scientists are testing several different contraception methods for men. These include:

- Pills, injections and implants with chemicals that act like natural hormones to signal:

    -The testicles to make fewer sperm.

    -To slow sperm down. Then, they can't get to the ovum to fertilise it.

    -To interrupt the growth of sperm. That way, the sperm do not mature enough to be able to fertilise an ovum.

- Pills that prevent ejaculation. That way no sperm escape to fertilise an ovum.

- Heat treatments of the testicles with ultrasound. The heat stops sperm production for several months.

Some methods have only been tested in animals. Many have already proved safe in animals. Those found safe in animals, scientists are now testing in men. These methods must prove safe and effective for men. Then they may be approved for sale.

Summing Up

- To prevent pregnancy, contraception must be used every time a man and woman have sex.

- Barrier methods prevent sperm from meeting an ovum.

- Spermicides kill sperm.

- Hormonal methods use chemicals that act like natural hormones to prevent pregnancy.

- IUDs hamper how sperm move. They prevent the sperm from reaching an ovum. They may also prevent a fertilised egg from implanting in the uterus.

Chapter Four
Safer Sex

STIs

Sex is a way to share love and caring. What no one wants to share is infections.

Several different infections can be passed to a partner during sex. That's why they are called sexually transmitted infections – STIs for short.

Many STIs are very dangerous. Some are possibly deadly. None are good for your body.

Some STIs can be easily cured. Others cannot. Many can affect a person's health for the rest of life.

People often don't know they have STIs. Some STIs have few or no symptoms. Or the symptoms go away quickly and the infection remains. Even without causing symptoms, STIs can cause long-lasting problems. And they can still spread infection. That's why it's important that partners always practice safer sex.

For details about STIs and their symptoms, see Table 2 on page 114.

'Some STIs can be easily cured. Others cannot. Many can affect a person's health for the rest of life.'

Entryways

STIs are caused by viruses or bacteria. The STI can be passed in an exchange of body fluids between partners. These may include semen, vaginal fluids or saliva. STIs enter the body through its openings. Possible entries include everything but the ears:

- Mouth.
- Vagina.
- Urethra.
- Anus.

During sex, STIs can also pass from the fluids into a partner's bloodstream through tiny tears in the vagina, the rectum, or even the mouth. Some STIs can pass through broken skin directly into the bloodstream. Cuts, insect bites, even small scrapes provide entry.

'Dirty' needles

Needles provide direct entry to the bloodstream. 'Dirty' needles, that is, needles that are not sterilised, can pass on an STI. This can include needles used for:

- Taking illegal drugs.
- Body piercings.
- Tattoos.

How a virus works

If a virus infects a healthy human cell, it hijacks the cell. It uses the cell's own ability to duplicate. The virus then makes copies of itself. These copies of the virus infect more healthy cells. As they multiply, the viruses spread infection through the body.

STI viruses may cause symptoms. Some may not. In either case, they can stay in a person's body long after any symptoms go away – often for a lifetime – A person with an STI virus can still pass it to any sex partners.

How vaccinations work

Vaccinations can prevent you getting some viruses. You were likely vaccinated as a child. That prevented you from getting diseases like the measles.

Vaccination enlists the human body's defense system to fight a virus. It trains a person's immune system to recognise the virus. The immune system then makes antibodies. Antibodies are special cells that attack infection.

Right now, there are vaccinations against only two STIs:

- Human papillomavirus – HPV for short. A papilloma is a wart. HPV may cause warts on men's and women's genitals.

▨ Hepatitis B – A disease that can seriously damage the liver.

If you are a girl between 12 and 18, you have likely been vaccinated against HPV. Recently, some medical experts have recommended boys also be vaccinated.

In general, hepatitis B is less of a problem in the UK than in other parts of the world. For that reason, vaccination is not usually recommended.

How bacteria work

We all have good bacteria in our bodies. For example, bacteria in the gut help digestion.

Bacteria that cause infection usually do it by making a toxin. After they enter the body, the bacteria multiply and spread the toxin.

How antibiotics work

Antibiotics either kill bacteria or slow their growth. They are designed to work only against infections caused by bacteria. They never work against infections caused by a virus. That's because viruses multiple very differently. You can see that in the section on page 42.

Mutants

Both viruses and bacteria mutate. Their traits can change over time. For this reason, vaccinations against some viruses are hard to design. The vaccination may work for a while. Then the virus mutates and the vaccination no longer works. The same thing happens when an antibiotic stops working against certain bacteria. Exposed to the same antibiotic repeatedly, the bacteria mutate. That makes them resistant to the effects of the antibiotic.

Parasites

As well as viruses and bacteria, there are also parasites that can be passed between sex partners. These are little creatures that live off the human body. (For details see Table 2, page 114.)

A little history on safer sex

The use of condoms for safer sex was first promoted in the 1980s. This was to control the spread of what came to be known as acquired immune deficiency syndrome – AIDS.

- Acquired, because people didn't inherit it, they got it.

- Immune deficiency, because it caused the immune system to fail.

- Syndrome, because it was not a single disease. It made people prone to many different diseases.

The AIDS epidemic began in 1981. The first eight cases were among gay men.

All victims of the epidemic were getting lots of very serious infections and cancers. And they were dying. It was two years before the virus causing AIDS was identified. It later came to be called HIV.

'HIV stands for human immunodeficiency virus: a virus that attacks the human immune system.'

HIV is a very fragile virus. It can't live in open air. No one can get HIV through casual daily contact with a person infected with HIV. Even hugging and sharing dishes are perfectly safe. It can only be passed on through sex.

HIV is a virus that attacks white blood cells. Usually the white blood cells in our bodies fight infection. But HIV damages them and makes them unable to defend against diseases. Unchecked, HIV was causing AIDS. It was destroying its victims' immune systems.

In 1983 the first cases of AIDS in women appeared. By that time gay groups were already promoting condom use for safer sex. But the disease quickly spread around the world. What began with eight cases in 1981 became a pandemic – a worldwide epidemic. By the end of 1985, 20,303 cases of AIDS had been reported. (Source: www.avert.org/aids-history-86.htm, accessed 2 Feb 2012.)

To control the pandemic, by the late 1980s safer sex for both men and women was promoted in most developed countries.

Much research was focused on AIDS. In 1986, the drug AZT was found to slow the action of HIV. By 1989 it was clear that AZT could actually prevent the progression from HIV to AIDS.

By the end of 2010, about 34 million people across the world were living with HIV. (Source www.actoronto.org/home.nsf/pages/hivaidsstatsworld, accessed 3 Feb 2012.)

Where things stand today

There are many new drugs to treat HIV and AIDS. The good news is:

- There are fewer new cases of HIV.

- Controlled with drugs, HIV no longer has to lead to AIDS.

- With effective drugs, fewer people with AIDS are dying of AIDS.

There is still no cure for AIDS. No vaccination has yet been made to fight the virus, HIV.

HIV's damage to the immune system means people with HIV can't fight infection. They are more likely to get sick. They are also more likely to get other STIs. Then they can pass those STIs on as well. For this reason, many other STIs are on the rise. That includes ancient STIs like syphilis and gonorrhoea.

Syphilis and gonorrhoea have existed for centuries. Both infections are caused by bacteria. They were untreaTable until the early 1940s. At that time penicillin was used for the first time. Penicillin and other antibiotic treatment since then, cured these two STIs. There were many fewer infections with syphilis and gonorrhoea.

Since 2000, both infections are on the rise. Gonorrhoea has recently become resistant to some antibiotics.

Safer sex is the best protection against STIs.

- It protects against HIV.

- Because HIV can lead to AIDS, it protects against AIDS.

- It protects against other STIs on the rise.

'Controlled with drugs, HIV no longer has to lead to AIDS.'

Safer sex methods and how they work

Safer sex uses barriers between partners. These prevent their bodily fluids from mixing. They can also prevent infected skin from touching. A couple must use a barrier every time. That way, an STI one partner may have should not pass to the other partner.

Barriers for safer sex

Whatever form of contraception a couple chooses, they must use barriers for safer sex. See chapters 3 and 9 for details about condoms.

Barriers that can be used for safer sex include:

Male condoms to cover the penis to form a barrier:

- Between the penis and vagina.
- Between the penis and the mouth.
- Between the penis and anus or rectum.

Female condoms to cover the vagina, cervix and vulva to form a barrier:

- Between the female genitals and penis.
- Between the female genitals and the mouth.

Dental dams are sheets of latex or rubber. They are often used during dental procedures, that's how they get the name. They can be used to cover the vulva or anus to form a barrier:

- Between the mouth and vulva.
- Between the mouth and anus.

Latex gloves cover the whole hand. Finger cots cover one or more fingers. Either gloves or finger cots will form a barrier:

- Between fingers and the penis.
- Between fingers and the female genitals.
- Between fingers and the anus or rectum.

'Using a barrier for safer sex is the best protection against STIs.'

These barriers protect from most STIs. But they do not always cover all possible areas of infection. Genital warts or sores may be in the groin or on the thighs. Some viruses may be on the skin and not be visible. See Table 2 on page 114 for more information.

It is important that only one partner wears one type of barrier. Two barriers rubbing against each other are more likely to break or slip.

Summing Up

- Using a barrier for safer sex is the best protection against STIs.

- Even without causing symptoms, STIs can cause long-lasting problems. And they can still spread infection.

- STIs can be passed in an exchange of body fluids between partners. STIs enter the body through its openings. They can also pass from the fluids into a partner's bloodstream through broken skin.

- HIV's damage to the immune system means people with HIV can't fight infection. They are more likely to get sick. They are also more likely to get other STIs and pass them on.

- Safer sex practices began in response to the AIDS epidemic in the 1980s.

Part Two

Your Choices

'We choose our joys and sorrows long before we experience them.'

Khalil Gibran

Modern sexual standards are unclear and confusing. You need to make your own decisions. First, get the facts you need to make the right choice for yourself. Weigh the information against your personal values. Above all, take the time to learn about yourself and the people you feel closest to. Make positive choices now to safeguard your health and happiness for the future.

Chapter Five

Emotions and Sexual Feelings

Emotions

Emotions are strong during your teen years. This is true for everyone.

There are lots of reasons. First, those new hormones are flooding your system. They make your moods swing. You might be sad and teary one day. The next day you may be wildly happy.

Second, you probably want more freedom. You might feel you have outgrown the rules at home and school. You have ideas of your own of what's right for you. You may struggle against the adults in your life. And your heightened moods may make those struggles more intense.

At the same time, life's a bit scary at this time. Everything about you is changing so fast. Sometimes it's hard to know who you are.

Sexual feelings

Sexual feelings and desires are a normal part of being human. Everyone has them. They are nothing to be ashamed of or embarrassed about. You likely had them when you were younger. But now they might be more intense. It will take you time to get used to them.

'Sexual feelings and desires are a normal part of being human. Everyone has them. They are nothing to be ashamed of or embarrassed about.'

Dating

Dating in groups or alone with someone can be fun. But not everyone is ready for dating at the same age. You may not be interested in the idea. Or you may not feel comforTable dating when your friends start.

Romance

You may look at your friends differently now. Maybe you notice a classmate you have never paid attention to before.

You may not be ready for romance. Often you need to know more about yourself first. We all have our own timeTable for love. Many of us first form close bonds as adults. But some teens get very close to one special person. Others may have a series of short relationships.

Close bonds of friendship or romance may stir new feelings. It may take time to learn to deal with these. You may feel jealous or angry. Try to talk about it. If you can't talk with the person who makes you feel this way, talk to someone you trust.

'For many people, sexual identities are not fully formed until adulthood. But some people say they knew at a very young age which sex they were more strongly attracted to.'

What's normal?

It's very normal for teens to feel attracted to people of the same sex. Many teens have sexual thoughts about people of their own sex. Some even have sexual experiences with those of their own sex. Does this mean they are gay? Probably not. For teens who aren't yet comforTable with sexual feelings, it may just feel safer with someone of the same sex.

For many people, sexual identities are not fully formed until adulthood. But some people say they knew at a very young age which sex they were more strongly attracted to.

Similarly, teens who think they may want to change their gender often already had those feelings as young children.

Remember that your teen years can be a time of turmoil. You're just getting used to your maturing body. You're dealing with new emotions. You likely feel awkward some of the time. All teens do. Don't be quick to label yourself. Take time to learn about yourself as a sexual being.

Talking with someone understanding can help you sort out confusing feelings you may have. If you don't feel you can talk with someone close to you, try talking with your health-care provider.

Sex and emotions

There is no such thing as casual sex. Sex brings up intense feelings. It exposes you emotionally. It is very easy to be hurt or to hurt your partner.

If you are close with one special person, honour what is good about your relationship. Don't feel pressured to make it more meaningful with sex.

Five good reasons not to rush into sex

1. Adding sex to a relationship is bound to change it. It can make it closer. But it may do the opposite.

2. It's very easy to be hurt emotionally.

3. Sex is not an inborn ability. People usually aren't very good at it at first. It takes time and maturity to learn.

4. Pregnancy is a risk. Teens, both girls and boys, are more fertile than adults.

5. STIs are a risk.

How to say 'No'

Your friends may brag about having sex. This may not be true. People often exaggerate such things. Even if they are true, it doesn't mean you have to do them. It's alright to say 'No'.

- Be clear in your own mind what your limits are.

- Make your limits clear. Don't make the other person guess.

- If you mean 'No', stand your ground.

- Don't be swayed by compliments or promises of love to act against your values.

- Don't let anyone pressure you into saying 'Yes' before you're ready. Say you want to think about it. If you're not sure, take time to talk and plan.

- Just because you said 'Yes' once, doesn't mean you have to say it again.

Sexual expression without intercourse

You can be physically very close to another person without intercourse. Kissing, cuddling, hugging, stroking and caressing are all ways to express your caring. You may learn more about your own sexual responses in this slow and easy way than if you feel pressured to have intercourse.

'You can be physically very close to another person without intercourse.'

The small drops of semen secreted before ejaculation carry sperm. Even those drops can cause pregnancy. Semen and vaginal secretions can carry STIs. If you are not using contraception and condoms for safe sex, avoid all contact between the penis and vagina. That includes touching or rubbing.

Self-pleasure

Exploring your sexual responses privately by yourself is a normal and healthy way to learn about your body. It's a safe way to release the strong sexual urges you may have. Learning about your sexual responses alone can keep them from complicating a relationship that may not be ready for sex.

Ideas

- Keep a journal. Track your emotions over a week.

- Ask your librarian to recommend a coming-of-age book. These are books about the teenage years. There are lots of them, both novels and biographies. Many are written by famous authors — after you read it, discuss the book with a friend or an adult.

- Ask an adult about his or her first crush.

- Ask an adult about how he or she fell in love for the first time.

Summing Up

- The teen years are a time of strong emotions.

- It's very normal for teens to feel attracted to people of the same sex. Talking with someone understanding can help you sort out any confusing feelings you may have.

- Sex exposes people emotionally. It's easy to be hurt.

- It is possible to be physically very close to another person without intercourse.

- Learning about your sexual responses alone can keep them from complicating a relationship that may not be ready for sex.

Chapter Six

Sex and the Media

The Internet

The Internet is a great resource. You can find just about anything you want online. And social media is a terrific way to connect with your friends. It's also a way to find people with common interests.

Privacy settings

Right now, perhaps the greatest threat to your privacy is your parents looking at your Facebook page. But to safeguard your privacy all round, keep these things in mind:

- Many browsers track every search you do. This is often called personalisation. It's designed to make it easier to reconnect with old sites you've visited. For the browser company, it allows them to collect data on your preferences. They can share that data with their advertisers. If you don't want a trail of everywhere you've been on the web, choose a browser that allows you to opt out of personalisation.

- Check Internet services' privacy policies. Search for the word 'share'. This will let you know how your data might be shared. It should also tell you if you can opt out of sharing.

- Use unique passwords and keep them to yourself.

- Choose your Internet 'friends' carefully. And limit your privacy settings to 'friends only'.

- Choose 'off-the-record' chat options when you don't want your posts to go any further.

'Choose your Internet "friends" carefully. And limit your privacy settings to "friends only".'

- Be aware of services that keep a permanent record of your posts. (For example, Facebook's Timeline.)

Online etiquette

The real world has rules of etiquette. It's a code of behaviour. The virtual world has its own approach to spelling. Its code of behaviour is less clear. Online there tends to be a psychological distance between people. This gives some false courage. They may say things they might not say in a crowded room. Or that they might not say to a person's face. They might misrepresent themselves, or spread falsehoods about someone else.

Use your real world code in your virtual dealings:

- Demand respect and be respectful of others.

- Don't share more information online than you would face-to-face.

- Trust your gut feelings: if you sense a post is mean or untrue, say so. And don't forward it.

- Take disagreements and personal matters out of the chat room. Correspond one-to-one via email or phone. If you know the person involved and feel safe, meet face-to-face. Issues usually resolve most easily in person.

Online reputations

Permanent online records

It's possible for the Internet to keep a permanent record of anything you put on it. This can come in very handy. You can retrieve a friend's address you might have misplaced. You can reconstruct a school assignment. But this permanent record can be a reputation killer.

Viral messages

Viral messages can also be reputation killers. They can spread to every address on the contact list of every recipient. All it takes is the click of the forward button. Then the message multiples geometrically.

Without privacy settings and good online etiquette, very personal postings can go viral. Rumours, photos and videos can take on a life of their own. Respect the reputation of others. Don't forward their personal information.

Safeguarding your reputation

Your online reputation is a combination of:

* Your own postings.

* Postings linked to you.

* Postings about you.

* Postings by others, pretending to be you.

You value your reputation. It will follow you out of school and into the workplace. Potential employers often check Facebook or other online pages.

As a teen, you will likely have more than one serious relationship. Your group of friends may change over time. What goes on between you and your current friends may later prove embarrassing.

Safeguard your reputation for now and the future.

* Use privacy settings.

* Follow good Internet etiquette.

* Represent your true self online.

* Think twice about their lasting effects before you post facts or photos.

* Review what others say about you. Use search engines to check the Internet, social networks, and blogs for your name.

'Safeguard your reputation for now and the future.'

Online safety

People with bad or bizarre behaviour on the street, have it online too. So, use your street smarts. If dealing with strangers on the Internet, be wary.

Mistrust those who:

* Are overly flattering.

- Offer gifts, money, or special deals.

- Say odd things.

- Want to talk about sex.

- Make you feel uncomforTable in any way.

Protect your privacy:

- Don't share your home address or the addresses of other places you spend time.

- Don't share your last name.

For your safety, be honest about your age. Limit other personal information you share. But try to find out as much as you can about the other person. Then consider if you believe it.

If you feel uncomforTable, log off.

If you think this person might be worth getting to know, spend several sessions online. Consider whether the person seems the same each time. Beware if the person seems too anxious to meet.

'For your safety, be honest about your age. Limit other personal information you share.'

Mobile phones

Mobile phones now mostly have direct access to the Internet. Your phone calls are still private. But text and Twitter messages can be forwarded. And anyone using your phone has access to your social network. Only share your phone with those you trust. Lock it if you are not using it.

Locator programs

Many mobile phones have locator programs. The programs use a global positioning system – GPS for short. The GPS locates your exact position on earth. This makes finding your way around easy. You can get step-by-step directions. Or you can get a photo of the place you are going on the Internet. You and your friends can find a meeting place.

Many mobile phone locator programs sync with your other services. These might include Facebook, chat rooms and Twitter. That means your location might be broadcast to everyone in your social network. This could include people you don't even know.

Safeguard your privacy. If your mobile phone syncs with social networking services:

▪ Turn off the function on the phone. Use each service's sharing tools instead.

▪ On each service, restrict your list of contacts to those you trust. This will reveal your location only to those on the list. Update your list regularly.

▪ Note that some services allow others to check your locations. Find out if your services do. Check the privacy policies for ways to opt out of that function.

Sexting and cybersex

Sexting and cybersex can be reputation killers. Safeguard your own reputation and those of others. Think twice before sending revealing photos or videos, or sexual comments via a mobile phone or the Internet.

▪ Once you press the 'send' button, there's no going back.

▪ Going viral: Consider how you might feel if the message or photo went to all your classmates, their parents, your teachers, or your workplace.

Art or porn?

The purpose of art is to display beauty or emotion. The naked human body is beautiful. Artists have made images of it through the ages. Museums are full of drawings, paintings and sculptures of naked bodies.

The purpose of pornography is to stimulate sexual excitement.

How porn differs from reality

If you watch porn, keep in mind:

- Breasts and penises are oversized. Big enough to make anyone feel inadequate.

- There's no foreplay, no tenderness.

- No one discusses or appears to use contraception or safer sex methods.

- The sex is often about power or violence.

- In sex between a man and a woman, the woman appears to be there to do whatever the man wants.

Sex in the real world is about connection and intimacy. It's a way to learn more about someone you care for.

'Sex in the real world is about connection and intimacy. It's a way to learn more about someone you care for.'

Ideas

- To find out how far your Internet reach is, send a simple message to your entire contact list requesting a 'yes' or 'no' answer. See how many answers you get.

- Plan an afternoon with three or four friends in the real world. Turn off your electronics. Does the conversation differ from online chat?

- Spend an afternoon in a museum. Look at paintings and sculptures of naked bodies.

Summing Up

■ Use your real-world values and code of behaviour in your virtual dealings.

■ Think twice about their lasting effects before you post facts or photos.

■ People with bad or bizarre behaviour on the street, have it online too. If dealing with strangers on the Internet, be wary.

■ Sexting and cybersex can be reputation killers.

■ Sex in the real world is about connection and intimacy.

Chapter Seven

Risk Taking

You'll be tempted to try new things and take risks. Taking risks is a way to test your independence. You're sure to make a few mistakes. That's part of growing up. Avoid the big ones:

- Learn to trust your gut reactions.

- Think ahead about the results of your actions. Be sure they agree with your own values.

- If you're not sure about something, get more information.

Brain changes and risk taking

Back in chapter 1 we talked about brain and hormone changes. These changes affect how teens view risk. The thrill-seeking part of your brain develops first. More rational decision-making powers won't fully develop until you are around 25 years old. That means you may not see the risks of some things you do. Add bursts of dopamine, the hormone that excites you, and you may act before you think.

Faced with new situations, keep these things in mind. Make it a habit to think twice before you act.

Brain changes and your values

Your teen years are a testing ground for your values. As your brain develops, you will think more deeply than as a child. Many of the new, deep thoughts you have will be about your personal values. You'll likely compare yours to those of your family and your friends. They may not be the same.

Use your values as a tool to judge risk. Make sure your actions reflect your values. That can help keep you and others safe.

Make up your own mind. Don't be swayed by what your friends say.

Trust gut reactions

Before you act, stop to check your gut reaction. If something feels wrong or unsafe, it probably is.

Get good information

To make good decisions, get good information. Learn ahead about the risks you may face as a teen. These may include:

- Pregnancy and unprotected sex.
- STIs and unprotected sex.
- Risks of alcohol and drugs.

Your friends or siblings may have a lot of information. Double check that it is correct. Even information adults share may not be.

The Internet has a lot of information. Not all websites are trustworthy. Just the website's name can be a clue whether it will be. Look for sites with scientific backing that are still easy to understand. Check several sites and compare the information.

Learn all you can about contraception and safer sex. Talk to your health-care professional. You can depend on that information.

Thinking ahead

It's often hard to make good decisions in the heat of the moment. Get into the habit of thinking things out ahead. If you have a date and think you might have sex, take condoms.

Safety in numbers

Don't go to parties alone. Arrange to go with friends. Friends you can trust. Agree ahead that you will look out for each other. Stay together. Don't let anyone leave alone or with someone not in your group.

If you think there will be drinking, agree that one of you will not drink. That person is in charge of the group's safety. The group needs to agree beforehand to listen to the sober one.

Remember – it is against the law to drink alcohol until you are 18. It's never a good idea to mix alcohol with dating. Things can easily get out of hand.

Alcohol

Alcohol is a part of many social activities. That includes parties, weddings and other celebrations. It's often an addition to meetings between friends. You will likely be offered alcohol even before you are of legal age. Learn to drink responsibly when it is legal for you to do so. Then you can enjoy the social aspects of drinking throughout your adult life.

How much alcohol in a drink?

A unit of alcohol is the measure of pure alcohol in a drink:

- Half pint of beer = 1 to 2 units.
- Medium glass of wine (175ml) = 2 units.
- Pub measure of spirits = 1 unit.
- Alcopops = 1.5 units.

Some safe drinking tips

- Eat before you drink and while you drink. Food in your stomach absorbs some of the alcohol. That way, less alcohol reaches your brain. Also, the food can protect your stomach lining.
- Control your pace. It takes your liver more than an hour to clear your body of one unit of alcohol. Don't outpace your liver.

- Drink water. It seems strange, but alcohol dehydrates you. It robs your body of the liquid it needs. Be sure to drink water if you drink alcohol. It will keep you hydrated. It will also lessen how much alcohol you drink.
- Know what you're drinking. The units of alcohol in a bottle are on the label. Check the label.

Mixing alcohol with energy drinks is dangerous. The caffeine in energy drinks masks the effects of the alcohol.

Drugs

Using drugs is risky.

There's no quality control for illegal drugs. Drug dealers may dilute them with dangerous fillers. Drugs can work differently each time. You won't know what to expect.

Prescription drugs are approved for specific uses. They are prescribed in specific doses. Used illegally in different doses, they can be dangerous.

'Eat before you drink and while you drink.'

Drugs, alcohol and your brain

Dopamine, the happiness factor

Back in chapter 1, we talked about dopamine. It's the hormone that makes you happy. So, you know that teens have an uneven supply. Drugs and alcohol signal the brain to make extra dopamine. The extra dopamine creates pleasure. Often teens seek that pleasure because their own supply of dopamine is low.

If a teen reguarly abuses drugs or alcohol, the brain supplies less natural dopamine. That means less natural happiness. This can lead to a bad cycle. The teen seeks the high of extra dopamine through further drinking or drug use.

The plastic brain

You'll remember from chapter 1, it's easy to develop new connections in your brain. Right now, your brain is plastic. That's good. You can learn new things easily and well. But your brain can make bad connections just as easily. Addictive patterns can become built-in. This happens much more easily for teens than adults. That's because their brains are plastic.

If you only socialise when you drink, your plastic brain makes that connection too. You may find it hard to relax in a group without a drink. Build healthy connections. Make sure you also get together with friends in settings where alcohol is not a focus.

The teen brain is a different brain

Alcohol does more damage to the teen brain than to the adult brain. Alcohol abuse can shrink parts of the developing brain. And it can damage connections between different brain parts. The memory center is still growing. So, the new memory cells are more sensitive. Alcohol abuse can keep those cells from maturing properly. That can lead to problems forming new memories. That, in turn, can affect how you learn.

Why drugs and alcohol don't mix with sex

Alcohol and drugs impair your judgement.

* You may do things you wouldn't do when sober.

* You may end up with someone you don't want to be with.

* You may not think to use a condom, risking STIs and pregnancy.

* You put yourself at risk of abuse.

To work to prevent pregnancy, the hormones in the pill must be in a girl's system daily. If she gets sick from drinking, the hormonal effects may be weakened. Pregnancy is a risk.

'Alcohol does more damage to the teen brain than to the adult brain. Alcohol abuse can shrink parts of the developing brain.'

If you plan to have sex, keep your wits. Avoid alcohol. You need to have a clear head to:

- Make good decisions about your sex life.
- Defend yourself from possible abuse.
- Be considerate of your partner.

Drink spiking

Drink spiking is a crime. It can happen at parties or at a pub. It can even happen on a date with someone you don't know well. When you are not looking, someone may add something to your drink. It may be someone who might want to take advantage of you sexually. Or someone who wants to rob you.

'Any sedative can put you at risk of abuse. That includes alcohol. It is also a sedative.'

Certain strong sedative drugs are known as date rape drugs. They slow down your reactions. Even not mixed with alcohol, they make you feel very drunk, very fast. In this state, you are at great risk of abuse. You are in physical danger. You can lose control or black out.

Common date rape drugs include Rohypnol, GHB and ketamine. But there are many others. All have many nicknames. They are colourless. They have no taste or smell, so you won't know anything is in your drink.

Any sedative can put you at risk of abuse. That includes alcohol. It is also a sedative. Someone with bad intentions can add large amounts of alcohol to your drink.

Protect yourself from drink spiking

- Stick with your friends. Watch out for each other.
- Be aware of who is near you and what they are doing.
- Drink from bottles or cans. Always open them yourself. Keep the opening covered with your hand.
- Keep your drink with you at all times. If you forget and leave it, pour it out.

- Never accept a drink from someone else. Never share drinks. Never drink from a punchbowl.

Signs of drink spiking

- Feeling drunk when you haven't had alcohol. Or feeling much drunker than you would expect when you have had alcohol.
- Blacking out.
- Memory loss.

If you think your drink has been spiked

- Get to a safe place, away from anyone you suspect may have spiked the drink.
- Find someone you trust to take you to the nearest hospital.
- If there is some of your drink left, take it as evidence.
- Provide a sample of your urine as soon as possible. Evidence of date rape drugs generally shows in your urine for only a few hours.
- Once you are physically safe, report the crime of drink spiking to the police.

If you think you have been sexually assaulted

- Go to a hospital or your doctor as soon as possible.
- Get tested for STIs and/or pregnancy.
- Report the crime to the police.

Ideas

- Make a list of the things that are most important to you.

- Think about where you get your information on topics like sex, drugs and alcohol. Consider whether these are reliable sources. Explore other sources.

- Think about which of your friends you would want to rely on in an emergency.

- Next time you are invited to a party, take food. It's always a welcome addition.

- Use your plastic brain: make a list of new skills you might like to learn. (For example, drawing, playing a musical instrument or a new sport.) Take a class or join a club to learn more.

- Plan an activity for a group of friends that doesn't include alcohol. (For example, a hike, a day at the beach, a skating party.)

Summing up

- Your decision-making powers won't fully develop until you are around 25 years old. You may not see the risks of some things you do.

- Your teen years are a testing ground for your values. Use your values as a tool to judge risk.

- To make good decisions, get good information.

- Make it a habit to think ahead.

- Teens may abuse alcohol and drugs to get a dopamine high because their own supply of dopamine is low.

- Alcohol does more damage to the teen brain than to the adult brain.

- If you plan to have sex, stay away from alcohol.

- Protect yourself from drink spiking.

Chapter Eight
Respect

Respect for yourself

You deserve respect. Decide how you want others to treat you. Never accept less. The people you spend time with should make you happy.

Respect for others

- Always value the worth of others.
- Respect what is private about a relationship.
- Never risk another person's safety.
- Try to know what others feel. Girls and boys often expect different things from each other. You may have to ask a few questions to know for sure.
- Don't push someone to do anything they don't want to do.
- Never take advantage of someone who has been drinking or using drugs.

Avoiding tricky situations

When you first begin to date, it can be confusing. Sometimes you may feel pressured to do things you don't want to do. Keep these things in mind:

- You never have to do anything that doesn't feel safe or good to you.
- You never have to go out with someone you don't like.
- If you're not sure about someone, go out in a group the first few times.
- Don't go to isolated spots, especially with someone you don't know well.

When someone is bad for you

- Stop seeing people you don't enjoy.
- Don't go out with someone who expects you to do things you don't want to do.
- If you can't break it off yourself, get help from someone you trust.

Signs of an abusive person

Learn the signs of an abusive personality. An abusive person may:

- Not care for your physical safety.
- Become scary or violent.
- Physically hurt you or threaten you.
- Pressure you for sex.

An abusive person may:

- Be very bossy.
- Often embarrass you or make fun of you.
- Spread rumors about you.
- Not let you have other friends.
- Check up on you, or spy on you.

An abusive person may:

- Become very jealous or possessive of you – jealousy is not love, it's control.
- Blame you or others for the way she or he acts.
- Threaten to hurt him/herself if you want to break up.

'Don't go out with someone who expects you to do things you don't want to do.'

When sex is abuse

Sex should always be a way to show deep caring for another person. Sex is abusive if it's used to dominate or humiliate you. This can happen with strangers, in families, or on dates. It's never your fault. If you're ever forced, tricked or bribed into doing something sexual you don't want to do, get help.

Unwanted advances

A touch on the shoulder can be a pleasant human connection. A hug can be comforting. Trust your gut feelings. You will likely be able to tell the difference between a friendly pat and a sexual advance. If you don't want to be touched, say so.

Someone's nice smile should make you feel happy. But if someone is looking up and down your body, they are probably thinking about sex. That will likely make you feel odd. If you're not interested in sex, make that clear:

- Look away.
- Get away.
- Tell the other person to go away.

What's a paedophile?

A paedophile is an adult who is sexually attracted to children or teens. The word comes from two Greek words: 'child' and 'love'. But what a paedophile does has nothing to do with love. It's sexual abuse.

Paedophiles have psychological problems. They often seek out jobs where they will have contact with young people. Many have an unusual ability to build trust with their victims. That means your usual gut reactions may not warn you of danger.

If you don't feel safe

Abuse can include physical attack or sexual abuse. Controlling or threatening behaviour is also abuse. If you don't feel safe, talk to someone you trust, or call one of the contacts listed in the help list.

If you are in immediate danger, always call the police.

Ideas

- Get together with friends and make lists of all the great things about each other. You may learn some good things about yourself you didn't know.

- Plan to do something special for someone you care about.

Summing Up

- Demand respect for yourself.
- Value the worth of others.
- You never have to do anything that doesn't feel safe or good to you.
- Sex should always be a way to show deep caring for another person.

Chapter Nine

Contraception: Power Over Your Future

Learn all you can

A pregnancy can short-circuit your chances in life. Contraception gives you power over your future. It gives you the control to avoid pregnancy until you are ready.

Even if you are not thinking about having sex, it's a good idea to learn about contraception. This way, you'll have the information when you need it. You'll make choices about contraception throughout your adult life.

Table 1 on page 108 has a summary of all methods. You can get more information from a parent, your health-care provider or a clinic.

How effective is each method?

There is a lot written about how effective different contraceptive methods are. Data on effectiveness of different methods is not included here. That's because most contraception failures are not due to the methods themselves. Most are because a couple:

▪ Forgot to use the method at least once.

▪ Used the method improperly at least once.

▪ Used a defective or out-of-date product at least once.

A method is most effective if it is:

- Available every time you need it.

- Easy to use every time you need it.

- A high quality product.

Plan ahead

Sex between a man and a woman without contraception always risks pregnancy. You'll remember from chapter 2, that there are 400 million sperm all aiming for one ovum.

Before you think about having sex, think about what form of contraceptive methods would work for you.

Start by getting good information.

'Before you think about having sex, think about what form of contraception methods would work for you.'

- Some methods are easier and safer for teens to use than others. Find out which suits your needs best.

- All contraceptive methods have some risk of not working. This is especially true if they are not used properly. Talk to a health-care provider. Get instructions on how to use contraception and how to reduce risks of failure.

- Some methods can have physical side effects. Find out which methods are safe for you.

Be prepared

Using contraception doesn't mean you have to have sex. But, you have a good chance to avoid pregnancy if you do have sex.

It may be a good idea to try out the method you've decided is best for you. Condoms, diaphragms and cervical caps come in different sizes. Make sure that you have the right size. All contraception is free through the NHS if you are 16 or older. If you are under 16, your health-care provider may be able to prescribe contraception for you.

Male condoms

Anyone of any age can buy condoms. Condoms are for sale at chemists', petrol stations and many supermarkets. If you're embarrassed to ask for them, buy them from a machine or online. The machines are often in public toilets.

Learn how to use a condom before you need one. Both boys and girls should practise. Boys can practise on themselves. Girls can use a banana. A cucumber works too. Follow the instructions on the condom wrapper. Learn how to slip the condom on and off without tearing it.

Make sure condoms have a BSI Kitemark or CE mark on the wrapper. That means they are good quality you can trust.

Keep condoms on hand. Keep them safe from damage. Store in a cool dry place.

Do not use a condom if:

* The condom is out of date. Look on the wrapper for the use-by date.

* The wrapper is damaged.

* The condom itself is torn, brittle, stiff, or sticky.

Many condoms have a lubricant. Lubricant makes them slippery. It reduces friction. That makes sex more pleasurable. Less friction also reduces the risk of the condom breaking. If a condom does not have lubricant, add a water-based lubricant.

Never use these lubricants with a condom:

* Petroleum jelly.

* Cold cream.

* Mineral oil.

* VegeTable oil.

These contain oil. Oil damages condoms.

A good fit is important. A condom that is too tight can break. A condom that is too big can leak.

'Make sure condoms have a BSI Kitemark or CE mark on the wrapper. That means they are good quality you can trust.'

Girls' contraception options

As a girl, you have many contraception options. Make an appointment with a health-care provider to discuss your choice.

If you think you may want to take the pill, try it out first. See how it makes you feel. Leave yourself time to choose another method if you decide against it.

To prevent pregnancy, the pill must start before you have sex. The exact timing depends on when you had your last period. Discuss the timing with your health-care provider.

You can be fit for a female condom, a diaphragm or cervical cap by a doctor or a nurse. Be sure to ask for instructions how to use the device. At home, practise inserting it into your vagina. Make sure it seals around your cervix. Practise until you're sure you are inserting it correctly.

Things to know

'Contraception
– use it
every time.'

Abstinence

Remember, deciding to abstain from, or not have, vaginal intercourse is like any other method:

- You and your partner have to talk about using it.
- You both have to co-operate and be comfortable using it.
- You have to use it every time.

If you and your partner use abstinence, keep talking. Renew your commitment to it. Review your decision. Plan ahead for other contraception if you change your minds.

Natural family planning

Natural family planning is not a good option for teens. The method calculates the infertile days in a woman's cycle. A couple needs to be trained in the method. The calculations are always based on a regular cycle. Teens' monthly cycles are mostly irregular. Even if they seem to be regular, they can change suddenly. It is not safe to trust the calculations.

In an emergency

Emergency contraception may protect against pregnancy if:

- You have sex without contraception.

- You forgot to take one or more contraceptive pills and have had sex.

- Your contraception method fails.

- A condom breaks, slips or leaks.

- A diaphragm or cervical cap slips.

Get information about emergency contraception right away. Call your health-care provider or a clinic.

There are different types of emergency contraception. See chapter 3 and Table 1 on page 108 for details about how each works.

Never use emergency contraception if you already are pregnant.

'Natural family planning is not a good option for teens.'

Hormonal methods

One hormonal method is a pill that must be taken within three days after a single act of unprotected sex. (No later than 72 hours.) With a prescription it is free, or if you are over 16 you can buy it at a chemist's.

The other hormonal method is a pill that must be taken within five days after a single act of unprotected sex. (No later than 120 hours.) This pill is only available on prescription. The NHS only recommends the pill for women over 18. That's because its safety hasn't been tested in younger women.

Copper IUDs

Copper IUDs are used as regular form of contraception. They can also be emergency contraception if inserted within five days of unprotected sex.

Your health-care provider as your ally

Your health-care provider can answer your questions about sex. You can trust the information. Anything you share about your health is kept private. This is the law.

Ideas

※ You should feel comforTable talking to your health-care provider about sexual matters. If you don't, now's the time to find a new one. You will want to consult with this person over the years.

※ Get familiar with the different forms of contraception. Start by reviewing chapter 3 and Table 1 on page 108.

※ Girls: Track your periods. You can use a regular pocket calendar. (Just make a mark on the day of the start of your period each month.) Or you can download a calendar from any number of Internet sites. (Search 'period calendar'.)

Summing Up

- Contraception gives you power over your future. It gives you the control to avoid pregnancy until you are ready.

- You'll make choices about contraception throughout your adult life.

- Most contraception failures are not due to the methods themselves. They happen because couples don't use the method. Or they use it improperly. Get instructions on how to use contraception and how to reduce risks of failure.

- Sex between a man and a woman without contraception always risks pregnancy.

- Some methods are easier and safer for teens to use than others. Find out which suits your needs best.

Chapter Ten
Responsible Sex

Protect yourself and your partner

As you read in chapter 4, STIs are not good for your body. And many can affect people for the rest of their lives. Table 2 on page 114 has details on specific STIs.

Protect your health now and for the future. Protect your partner's health. For safer sex, use a contraceptive barrier every time. See the list of barriers on page 46. Use one for whatever type of sex you have.

Many barriers are made of latex. People with allergies to latex can get them made of other materials.

'Condoms are the only form of contraception that protect against STIs.'

Why they call it safer sex

Protecting against STIs is called safer sex because it's much safer than without protection.

▓ If your partner won't use a barrier, protect yourself – don't have sex.

▓ Don't have sex with a stranger – it's dangerous.

Choose your partner carefully

The first and most important step for safer sex is to know your partner. Take time to get to know each other well. Ask yourself, is this person:

▓ Considerate of me?

▓ Honest in daily life?

▓ Concerned about health?

Avoid risky partners

Some people have a lifestyle that puts them at greater risk of STIs. Learn to judge possible partners before you get involved.

Find out:

* How many sex partners has this person had?

* Did this person use safer sex with past partners?

* Has this person used needles to take drugs or had partners who did?

* Has this person ever had an STI?

Regular health checks are a part of safer sex

If you are sexually active, get check-ups at least once a year. This protects you and your partner. You may have no symptoms. But a medical exam, blood tests, or other tests can detect STIs.

If you think you have an STI

If you think you have been exposed to an STI, get tested right away. It's important to prevent passing it on. Many STIs can be treated quickly.

As we said in chapter 4, many STIs may have no symptoms. Or the symptoms may go away quickly. Even if there are no symptoms or they go away, an STI can still be passed on. That's why testing is so important.

Some STIs do have symptoms. A detailed list is provided in Table 2 on page 114. Many share similar symptoms. If you have any of these symptoms, get tested right away:

* Burning or stinging when you urinate.

* Discharge from your genitals or anus. (For women this only includes a change from your normal vaginal discharge.)

* Sores, blisters or warts on your genitals, mouth, anus, buttocks or thighs.

* Painful, swollen or sore genitals.

- Vaginal bleeding after sex.
- Swollen glands.

Test results

Don't have sex with anyone until you get the test results. If you have an STI, contact any partners you've had. They need to get tested too.

If you have an STI that can be treated, finish any treatment that is prescribed. Then ask for medical advice if you should get retested after treatment. Resume sexual activity only after you are sure you cannot infect your partner.

STI viruses

Right now there are only vaccinations against two STI viruses: HPV and hepatitis B. (See details in chapter 4 or Table 2 on page 114) Vaccinations only work against STI viruses if you don't already have the virus.

Some viruses your body can cure itself. If you have a strong immune system, it can fight the virus and get rid of it. For example, some mild types of HPV, which cause genital warts, may go away. It may take time though. You'll need to get retested to make sure you no longer have the virus.

Some STI viruses don't go away. Get medical advice on how to best protect your partner.

A word about spermicides

Spermicides used with a barrier method are good contraception. Most contain a chemical called nonoxynol-9. Research shows that nonoxynol-9 can irritate and cause small cuts in the skin. The cuts can provide HIV entry to the bloodstream. This is particularly true for anal sex. This is because the skin lining the rectum is quite fragile. It's more likely to get cut with friction. For this reason, spermicides should never be used during anal sex.

The vagina has natural lubrication. It is less prone to these small cuts. The research seems to show that with vaginal sex, the risk of getting HIV is only high if nonoxynol-9 is used many times a day. You will need to weigh the risk of pregnancy against the risk of HIV.

If your risk of HIV might be high, choose a method of contraception other than spermicide. Be sure to use condoms for safer sex. Some condoms are pretreated with spermicide. Make sure you use the kind without spermicide.

Contraception and romance

In books, movies and on TV, contraception is almost never mentioned during romantic scenes. In real life it is. Couples who care about each other talk about contraception. They plan to get it before they have sex. They share the responsibility and expense for contraception.

'If you are mature enough to think about having sex, you are mature enough to use contraception.'

■ If you are mature enough to think about having sex, you are mature enough to use contraception.

■ The decision to use contraception is a mature decision. If you and your partner can't talk about contraception, you are not ready to have sex.

■ If you are too embarrassed to talk about contraception, you risk your own future and your partner's.

The talk

Sex is something to share only if you have planned ahead. You and your partner must agree it's right for you. Talk to each other.

It's hard to talk about sex. It can help to practise ahead what you'll say. Write it down or plan it in your head.

Things to discuss:

■ How you feel about each other.

■ Whether it's the right time for each of you, and your relationship, to have sex.

■ What contraceptive methods you think will work best for you as a couple.

■ Your commitment to safer sex.

92

Safer sex and romance

You can't tell who is infected with an STI. Even someone you love very much may be. Often people may not know if they have an STI.

You may be tempted to stop using condoms if you have a very close partner for a long time. But if your partner is infected, he or she will still be infected. If you care for each other, show that caring by always practising safer sex. Think of it as a gift of love.

The learning curve

It takes time to learn to be a good lover. Take it slow. Indulge in foreplay. Learn about your partner's body. Explore all those nerve endings. Let each other know what feels good. Talk about it.

It also takes time to learn about relationships. That includes learning:

- How to be together.

- How to be apart.

- When someone needs time alone or time with family.

- How to express your needs and honor your partner's needs.

- Talk about what works in and out of bed.

'If you care for each other, show that caring by always practising safer sex.'

Ideas

- Set up a regular schedule of health check-ups for now and the future.

- Learn about the different kinds of STIs and their symptoms by reviewing Table 2 on page 114.

- Next time you watch a movie with sex, check:

    -Is there foreplay. How long does it last?

    -Does either partner mention contraception or safer sex practices?

- Make a list of the traits you look for in a partner.

Summing up

- For safer sex, use a barrier (male or female condom or dental dam) every time.

- The first and most important step for safer sex is to know your partner. Take time to get to know each other well.

- Regular health checks are a part of safer sex. They protect you and your partner.

- If you think you have been exposed to an STI, get tested right away.

- Sex is never one-sided. It always involves two people and many of their deepest feelings.

- It's important for a couple to talk together. Plan ahead for contraception and safer sex practices.

- It takes time to learn to be a good lover.

Glossary

Abstinence
Avoidance of sexual intercourse.

AIDS
Short for acquired immune deficiency syndrome, caused by the STI HIV.

Anal sex
Intercourse with the anus and rectum.

Antibiotic
A drug that kills bacteria or slows their growth.

Antibodies
Special cells of the body's immune system that attack infection.

Anus
The outside opening of the rectum.

AZT
Short for azidothymidine, a drug that can prevent the progression from HIV to AIDS.

Bacteria
Infect the human body by multiplying and spreading a toxin.

Barrier method
Blocks sperm from reaching an ovum and/or blocks STIs from infecting a partner.

BSI Kitemark
Proof that the British Standards Institute has tested the product and it conforms to their standards.

CE
Proof that a product meets European Community legal requirements.

Cervical cap
Barrier method of contraception that covers a woman's cervix.

Cervix
The opening to a woman's uterus from her vagina.

Circumcision
The removal of the foreskin of the penis. Usually done when a boy is an infant. Sometimes is part of a religious ceremony.

Circumcised penis
A penis with the foreskin removed.

Clitoris
A small, sensitive part of the female genitals, whose primary function is to create sexual pleasure.

Condom
A thin rubber sheath worn on the penis during sex as a contraceptive and to protect against STIs.

Contraception
A method that prevents pregnancy from happening.

Contraceptive implant
A hormone-based method of contraception where a strip of plastic containing a hormone that prevents ovulation is inserted under the skin.

Contraceptive injection
A method of preventing pregnancy by injecting a hormone into a woman to prevent ovulation.

Contraceptive patch
A sticking plaster that is applied to a woman's skin containing a hormone that is released into the bloodstream, which prevents pregnancy.

Cowper's glands
Male sex glands below the prostate, on the sides of the urethra. Make a slippery fluid that neutralises any acid in the urethra before the semen travels through it.

Cybersex
Sharing revealing photos or acting out sex online.

Date rape drugs

Drugs that slow down your reactions and make you feel very drunk, very fast, leaving you at great risk of abuse.

Diaphragm
Barrier method of contraception that fits inside a woman's vagina.

Dopamine
A hormone that makes people happy and excited.

Drink spiking
Putting a date rape drug in a drink.

Ejaculation
When semen is ejected from the penis, usually accompanied by a male orgasm.

Embryo
The earliest stage of development up to eight weeks.

Emergency contraception
A form of contraception taken after unprotected sex to help prevent pregnancy.

Epididymis
Long tubes that coil behind the testicles. The epididymis acts like a storage tank. It holds the sperm that the testicles make. It's here that the sperm mature.

Erectile tissue
Spongy tissue in male and female genitals with spaces where blood flows during sexual excitement.

Erection
When the penis has become hard or rigid.

Fallopian tubes
Tubes in a woman's body that connect her ovaries to her uterus.

Fertilisation
The meeting of a sperm and an ovum.

Female condom
A form of contraception that fits inside a woman's vagina.

Foetus
The stage of development from nine weeks until birth.

Foreplay
Sexual activity, such as kissing, touching etc., that precedes intercourse.

Foreskin
A hood of skin that covers the head of an uncircumcised penis.

Gene
What determines how family traits are passed from parent to child.

Genitals
Sex organs.

GHB
Short for gamma-hydroxybutyric acid. A sedative drug sometimes used to spike drinks. Known as a 'date rape drug'.

Glands
Body organs that produce hormones, the chemical messages to signal changes in the body.

Gonorrhoea
An STI caused by bacteria.

Groin
Area between the legs.

Growth hormone
A chemical message produced by the pituitary gland. Controls how fast and how tall you grow.

hCG
Short for human chorionic gonadotropin. The chorion is the outside covering of the embryo. A gonadotropin is a hormone that sends signals to sex glands. hCG is what is measured by a pregnancy test.

Hepatitis B
An STI that can seriously damage the liver.

HIV
Short for human immunodeficiency virus. An STI that attacks the human immune system and can lead to AIDS.

Hormones

Natural chemical messages. Produced by glands. Travel through the bloodstream to signal changes in the body. From the Greek word 'to urge' or 'to spur on'.

HPV

Short for human papillomavirus, an STI that causes warts on the genitals.

IUD

Short for intrauterine device. Fits inside the uterus and prevents pregnancy.

IUS

Short for intrauterine system. Similar to an IUD, it fits inside the uterus, but has progesterone to prevent pregnancy.

Ketamine

A sedative drug sometimes used to spike drinks. Known as a 'date rape drug'.

Labia

Soft flesh on each side of a woman's opening to her vagina. From the Latin word for 'lips'.

Lubricant

A gel or cream that makes a surface slippery and reduces friction.

Melatonin

A hormone that makes people sleepy.

Mini pill

A progesterone-based method of contraception.

Natural family planning

Calculating the infertile days in a woman's monthly cycle. Used as a method of contraception.

NHS

Short for National Health Service.

Nonoxynol-9

A chemical used in most spermicides.

Oestrogen

Sex hormone produced by the ovaries.

Oral sex
Exploration of a partner's genitals with the mouth.

Orgasm
An intense feeling of sexual excitement.

Ova
Plural of ovum (see below.)

Ovaries
A girl or woman's main sex glands that contain a lifetime's supply of ova.

Ovulation
The ovum's trip from the ovary down the fallopian tube to the uterus. The time when a woman is fertile.

Ovum
A single human egg. An ovum is the size of the full stop at the end of this sentence.

Paedophile
An adult who is sexually attracted to children or teens.

Pandemic
A worldwide epidemic. From a Greek word that means 'of all the people'.

Penicillin
The first antibiotic.

Penis
A man's sex organ, serves the double purpose of carrying semen and urine out of the body.

Period
The female monthly cycle. Also known as menstruation.

Personalisation
An Internet browser's program to track every search and collect data on a user's preferences.

The pill
Hormone-based method of contraception.

Pituitary gland
The 'master' gland in charge of all the body's glands.

Placenta
The embryo/foetus' life support center throughout pregnancy.

Porn
Short for pornography.

Pornography
Words or images intended to stimulate sexual excitement.

Progesterone
Sex hormone produced by the ovaries.

Prostate
Male sex gland that bridges the urethra. Adds fluid to semen to give sperm energy.

Puberty
The time when a child's body changes to an adult's.

Pubic hair
Hair that grows around the genital area.

Pubic mound
Pillow-like flesh that covers the pubic bone.

Rectum
The end portion of the bowels.

Rohypnol
A sedative drug sometimes used to spike drinks. Known as a 'date rape drug'.

Safer sex
The use of barriers to avoid the spread of STIs.

Scrotum
The pouch of skin that holds the testicles.

Sedative
A substance that slows down normal reactions.

Self-pleasure
Exploration of your own body's sexual responses.

Semen
The liquid that transports sperm.

Seminal vesicles
Attached to the sperm ducts below the bladder, they add sugary fluid to semen to give sperm energy.

Sexting
Sending revealing photos or sexual messages by mobile phone.

Sperm
Microscopic male sex cells that can fertilise ova.

Sperm ducts
Tubes that carry sperm to a man's urethra.

Spermicide
A substance used for contraception that kills sperm.

Sterilisation
Surgery for permanent contraception. Almost never possible to reverse.

STI
Short for sexually transmitted infection. That is, an infection that is passed on during sexual activity.

Syphilis
An STI caused by bacteria.

Testicles
A man's main sex glands that produce sperm.

Testosterone
Sex hormone produced by the testicles.

Trimesters
The three stages of a pregnancy.

Umbilical cord
Connection between an embryo and the pregnant woman. Carries oxygen and nutrients to the embryo and removes wastes from the embryo.

Uncircumcised penis
A penis with a foreskin.

Urethra

A tube that runs from the bladder and carries urine out of the body. In a man it also carries semen out of the body.

Uterus

Pear-shaped organ in a woman's body where a foetus can grow.

Vaccination

Trains a person's immune system to recognise and attack a virus.

Vagina

The passage leading from a woman's vulva to her cervix and uterus.

VCF

Vaginal contraceptive film, a spermicide.

Viral messages

Internet postings that multiply out of control and spread to too many people.

Virus

An infection that multiplies inside human cells.

Vulva

A woman's outside sex organs.

Wet dreams

Dreams during which a boy or man ejaculates semen.

Appendix

Contraceptive Choices

As you read in chapter 10, the effectiveness of a method of contraception often depends on whether it's used properly. As you read this Table, consider if a method fits with your lifestyle. Remember, a method is most effective if it is:

- Available every time you need it.
- Easy to use every time you need it.
- A high quality product.

Methods that don't fit a teen's lifestyle are not included here:

- Sterilisation, because it is a permanent form.
- Natural family planning, because it is undependable for teens. A girl's monthly cycle is likely to be irregular. Her infertile times can't be accurately calculated.

Table 1 Contraceptive Choices

Contraceptive and How it Works	How to Use
Cervical cap	
Fits over a woman's cervix. Suction keeps the cap on her cervix. The cap blocks the man's sperm from reaching her uterus.	First, the woman must make an appointment to have the cap fitted by a doctor or nurse. **Used with spermicide:** The cap should be filled 1/3 full with spermicide gel or cream. To assure suction keeps the cap on the woman's cervix, no spermicide should be used on the rim. For some types of caps, the woman should insert extra spermicide in her vagina after putting in the cap. This is done with an applicator.
Combined pill	
Pill with chemicals that act like natural oestrogen and progesterone to prevent pregnancy by: ▪ Preventing ovulation. ▪ Blocking the cervix with mucus. ▪ Thinning the lining of the uterus.	First, the woman must make a medical appointment to get the pill. If she has certain medical conditions, it may not be a good choice.
Diaphragm	
A dome with a flexible rim around the bottom. Fits inside a woman's vagina. It covers the woman's cervix to block the man's sperm from reaching her uterus. The flexible rim holds the diaphragm in place and keeps sperm from leaking around the edges. Made of latex or silicone.	First, the woman must make an appointment to have the diaphragm fitted by a doctor or nurse. Spermicide gel or cream is spread inside the dome and around the rim. This should kill any sperm that get around the rim of the diaphragm.
Female condom	
A pouch, open at one end, with rings at one or both ends, fits inside a woman's vagina. One ring holds it in place against her cervix. The open end of the pouch covers her labia. It blocks the man's sperm from reaching her uterus. Made of polyurethane.	Used with spermicide. The spermicide goes on the outside of the closed end. If the condom breaks or leaks, the spermicide should kill any sperm.

Timing	Things to Know if You Choose this Method
Cervical cap	
The cap can be put in up to 3 hours before having sex. That's how long the spermicide will work. If the couple has sex more than once, the woman must insert more spermicide into her vagina beforehand. The cap must stay in place 6 hours after sex. That makes sure no live sperm get by the cap rim when it is removed.	Inserting a cap takes practice. Take time to learn. Be sure you can fit it around your cervix. Make sure you can do this perfectly before you depend on it for contraception. A cap will last several years if well cared for. After you remove it, wash it with a mild soap that has no perfume. Air dry and store in its case. Check the cap regularly for holes or weak spots. Do this by holding it up to the light. Also check for splits around the rim. Do not leave the cap in for more than 48 hours.
Combined pill	
A woman must take the pill on a regular schedule throughout each month. There are many different brands. The schedule varies with different brands. It can take several days after a woman first takes the pill to be protected from pregnancy. A health-care provider can advise on the exact timing. Another method of contraception should be used in the meantime.	There's a chance of pregnancy even if you forget just one pill. Plan a regular time in your daily schedule to take your pill. If you vomit or have diarrhoea, the hormones in the pill may not reach your bloodstream. There's a chance of pregnancy during that month. Use another method of contraception. If you take other drugs or herbal products, some can make the pill ineffective. There's a chance of pregnancy while you take the drug or herbal product and for a time afterwards. Use another method of contraception.
Diaphragm	
The diaphragm can be put in up to 3 hours before having sex. That's how long the spermicide will work. If the couple has sex more than once, the woman must insert more spermicide into her vagina. The diaphragm must stay in place 6 hours after sex. That makes sure no live sperm escape the diaphragm's rim when the diaphragm is removed.	Inserting a diaphragm takes practice. Take time to learn. Be sure you can fit it around your cervix. Make sure you can do this perfectly before you depend on it for contraception. A diaphragm will last up to 2 years if well cared for. After you remove it, wash it with a mild soap that has no perfume. Air dry and store in its case. Check the diaphragm regularly for holes or weak spots. Do this by holding it up to the light. Also check for splits around the rim. Do not leave a diaphragm in for more than 24 hours.
Female condom	
A woman can insert the female condom up to 3 hours before having sex. That's how long the spermicide will work. The woman should remove the female condom right after sex. While removing it, she should twist the open end closed, so not to spill semen. The condom should be thrown in the bin. Never reused.	It helps to direct the man's penis into the condom. This avoids his penis sliding outside the condom. Never use together with a male condom. That increases the chance of breakage.

Contraceptive and How it Works	How to Use
Implant	
Flexible and about the size of a matchstick, the implant has chemicals that act like natural progesterone. It prevents pregnancy by: ▦ Preventing ovulation. ▦ Blocking the cervix with mucus. ▦ Thinning the lining of the uterus.	First, the woman must make a medical appointment to get the implant. If she has certain medical conditions, the contraceptive implant may not be a good choice. A doctor or nurse inserts the implant under the skin of the woman's upper arm.
Injection	
An injection into a muscle with chemicals that act like natural progesterone to prevent pregnancy by: ▦ Preventing ovulation. ▦ Blocking the cervix with mucus. ▦ Thinning the lining of the uterus. ▦ Usually the injection is given in the arm or buttocks.	If a woman has certain medical conditions, the contraceptive injection may not be a good choice. She will need regular medical appointments to get the shot.
IUD	
T-shaped and about 6 centimetres long, it fits inside a woman's uterus. It hampers sperm's movement, so they can't fertilise an ovum. May also prevent a fertilised egg from implanting in the uterus. Made of plastic or copper.	First, the woman must make an appointment to have the IUD inserted. A doctor or nurse inserts it through the opening of her cervix into her uterus.
IUS	
T-shaped and about 6 centimetres long. It fits inside a woman's uterus. Unlike a regular IUD, it contains chemicals that act like natural progesterone. It prevents pregnancy by: ▦ Blocking the cervix with mucus. ▦ Thinning the lining of the uterus. It may also prevent ovulation.	First, the woman must make a medical appointment to get the IUS inserted. If she has certain medical conditions, the IUS may not be a good choice. A doctor or nurse inserts the IUS through the opening of a woman's cervix into her uterus.
Male condom	
▦ A thin sheath the size and shape of a penis fits over the man's penis and traps sperm ▦ Made of latex, polyisoprene, or polyurethane	Keep condoms on hand. Used with spermicide: Some are pretreated with spermicide. For those that are not, the woman should insert spermicide into her vagina before having sex. If the condom breaks or leaks, the spermicide should kill any sperm. The male condom comes rolled in a small package. The man unrolls the condom over his erect penis. Lubricant reduces friction and the risk of the condom breaking. Some condoms are prelubricated. If adding lubricant, use only water-based lubricant.

Timing	Things to Know if You Choose this Method
Implant	
The implant can stay in place for up to 3 years to prevent pregnancy. It can be removed by a doctor or nurse at any time. If a woman gets the implant during the first 5 days of her period, she may be protected against pregnancy right away. At any other time of the month, she will not be protected from pregnancy for several days. The doctor or nurse can advise on the exact timing. Another method of contraception should be used in the meantime.	Certain drugs and herbal products can affect how well the implant works to prevent pregnancy. Be sure to review any drugs or herbal products you take with your health-care provider. For continued protection from pregnancy, it is very important to have the implant replaced on schedule.
Injection	
A woman gets the injection once every 8 or 12 weeks. How often depends on the brand. If a woman gets the injection during the first 5 days of her period, she may be protected against pregnancy right away. At any other time of the month, she will not be protected from pregnancy for several days. The doctor or nurse can advise on the exact timing. Another method of contraception should be used in the meantime.	If you have side effects, they will likely last for the whole time the injection is effective. They may even last several weeks after the injection has worn off.
IUD	
The IUD can safely stay in the uterus for several years. A woman can get it removed if she wants to get pregnant.	Not a good option if you are at risk for STIs. Once the IUD is inserted, there is nothing else to do. That makes it a good option for teens. May cause heavier monthly flow and cramping.
IUS	
The IUS is inserted within 7 days of the start of a woman's period. Once inserted, it prevents pregnancy for up to 5 years. It can be removed at any time.	Not a good option if you are at risk for STIs. In the first 3 to 6 months, may cause irregular, heavy periods, or spotting between periods. After about a year, it's possible you may have no periods at all. Your period will return if you have the IUS removed.
Male condom	
It's important the man's penis doesn't touch the woman's vagina before the condom is in place. Even small droplets of semen secreted before ejaculation carry sperm. When the man withdraws his penis from the woman's vagina he must hold the base of the condom tight when he does this. While his penis is still erect, he removes the condom without spilling semen. The condom should be thrown in the bin. Never reused,	A good fit is important. A condom that is too tight can break. A condom that is too big can leak. Never put a second condom over the first. That increases the chance of breakage. For the same reason, never use a male condom and a female condom together. Keep condoms in a cool, dry place. Check for BSI Kitemark or CE mark on the wrapper. Don't use after use-by date. Check for damage before using.

Contraceptive and How it Works	How to Use
Mini pill	
Pill with chemicals that acts like natural progesterone to prevent pregnancy by: ▪ Blocking the cervix with mucus. ▪ Thinning the lining of the uterus. The mini pill usually does not prevent ovulation.	First, the woman must make a medical appointment to get the mini pill. If she has certain medical conditions, it may not be a good choice.
Patch	
A sticking plaster that releases chemicals that act like natural–oestrogen and progesterone. Hormones are absorbed through the skin and into the bloodstream. Prevents pregnancy by: ▪ Preventing ovulation. ▪ Blocking the cervix with mucus. ▪ Thinning the lining of the uterus.	First, the woman must make a medical appointment to get the patch. If she has certain medical conditions, the patch may not be a good choice.
Spermicides	
Spermicides kill sperm. They come in the following forms: ▪ Gel or cream. ▪ Foam. ▪ Vaginal contraceptive film (VCF). ▪ Suppositories.	Spermicides work best to prevent pregnancy when used together with a barrier method. When used alone, a woman can insert the spermicide into her vagina before sex using the applicator. She should insert it deep in her vagina, close to her cervix.
Vaginal ring	
A flexible plastic ring with about a 5-centimetre opening that releases chemicals that act like natural oestrogen and progesterone. Hormones are absorbed into the bloodstream. Prevents pregnancy by: ▪ Preventing ovulation. ▪ Blocking the cervix with mucus. ▪ Thinning the lining of the uterus.	First, the woman must make a medical appointment to get the ring. If she has certain medical conditions, the ring may not be a good choice. A woman can insert the vaginal ring into her vagina herself. The exact position doesn't matter.

Timing	Things to Know if You Choose this Method
Mini pill	
It's extremely important that the mini pill is taken at exactly the same time each day. Otherwise there's a chance of pregnancy. It can take several days after you first take the mini pill to be protected from pregnancy. Your health-care provider can advise on the exact timing. Another method of contraception should be used in the meantime.	The exact time you take the pill each day is critical to protect against pregnancy. If you have an irregular school, work, or sleeping schedule, the mini pill is probably not a good choice. If you do choose to take the mini pill, consider setting a daily alarm. This can keep you on schedule.
Patch	
A woman wears one patch a week for three weeks. She skips the fourth week and wears no patch. The fourth week is the week of her period.	Except for the fourth week during your period, any 48 hours without the patch puts you at risk of pregnancy. If you forget to replace a patch or lose one, use another method of contraception until your next period.
Spermicides	
Most spermicides must be placed in the vagina at least 15 minutes before sex. That gives them time to dissolve. Packet instructions give exact timing. If the couple has sex more than once, the woman must insert more spermicide into her vagina.	Spermicides used with a barrier method are good form of contraception. Most contain a chemical called nonoxynol-9. Research shows that nonoxynol-9 can irritate and cause small cuts in the skin. The cuts can provide HIV entry to the bloodstream. This is particularly true for anal sex. Spermicides should never be used during anal sex. The research seems to shows that with vaginal sex, the risk of getting HIV is only high if nonoxynol-9 is used many times a day. If your risk of HIV might be high, choose a method of contraception other than spermicide. Be sure to use condoms for safer sex. Some condoms are pretreated with spermicide. Make sure you use the kind without spermicide.
Vaginal ring	
The woman inserts the ring at the start of her period. It stays in place for 3 weeks. That way, she's protected from pregnancy right away. After that, the woman removes the ring herself. For continued contraception she inserts a new ring at the start of her next period. If a woman inserts the ring at any other time of the month, she will need another method of contraception for several days. A health-care provider can advise on exact timing.	If the ring is out of your vagina for more than 3 hours there's a chance of getting pregnant. You will need to use another method of contraception for several days. Check with your health-care provider for exact timing. Store rings at room temperature, out of direct sunlight. Don't use after use-by date.

Contraceptive and How it Works	How to Use
Emergency contraceptive pill	
Like regular contraceptive pills, emergency contraceptive pills have chemicals that act like natural hormones. They prevent pregnancy by: ▨ Delaying ovulation. ▨ Thinning the lining of the uterus.	To be used for emergency contraception only. A woman should contact her health-care provider or a clinic as soon as possible after: ▨ Unprotected sex. ▨ Contraception failure.
Emergency copper IUD	
The same IUD used for regular contraception. Prevents pregnancy if inserted after unprotected sex. ▨ Hampers sperm's movement. ▨ Thins the lining of the uterus.	A woman should contact her health-care provider or a clinic to have the IUD inserted as soon as possible after: ▨ Unprotected sex. ▨ Contraception failure.

Timing	Things to Know if You Choose this Method
Emergency contraceptive pill	
One method is a pill that must be taken within 3 days after a single act of unprotected sex -- no later than 72 hours. The other method is a pill that must be taken within 5 days after a single act of unprotected sex -- no later than 120 hours.	Not meant as a routine form of contraception. Never use emergency contraception if you already are pregnant.
Emergency copper IUD	
Must be inserted within 5 days of unprotected sex.	Never use as emergency contraception if you already are pregnant. Once inserted, the IUD will provide long-term contraception.

Table 2 STI Facts

STI Name	Type of STI			Description
	Virus	Bacteria	Parasite	
Chlamydia		X		Untreated, chlamydia can cause infertility in women and, very rarely, also in men. That is, it damages their reproductive organs so they are unable to have children.
				Chlamydia often causes no symptoms. Possible symptoms, which may be mild, include:
				▓ Discharge from the penis or vagina.
				▓ Pain when urinating.
				▓ Swelling of the rectum.
				▓ Throat infection.
Gonorrhoea		X		Symptoms:
				In women:
				▓ Bleeding during or after vaginal intercourse.
				▓ Yellow or bloody vaginal discharge.
				▓ Pain or burning when urinating.
				▓ Cramps and pain.
				▓ Bleeding between periods.
				▓ Vomiting or fever.
				In men:
				▓ Discharge from the penis.
				▓ Burning when urinating.
				▓ Pain or swelling of the testicles.
				Symptoms of anal infection:
				▓ Discharge from the rectum.
				▓ Anal itching.
				▓ Painful, bloody bowel movements.
				It is possible to have the infection for several months with no symptoms.
				Untreated, gonorrhoea can cause infertility in both men and women. It can also cause serious infections of the joints, heart valves and brain.
Hepatitis B	X			Hepatitis B causes a serious disease of the liver. In general, hepatitis B is less of a problem in the UK than in other parts of the world.
				Symptoms:
				▓ Yellow skin or yellowed whites of the eyes.
				▓ Tiredness.
				▓ Loss of appetite, stomach pain, nausea, or vomiting.
				▓ Fever.
				▓ Dark urine.
				▓ Pain in the joints.

Diagnosis and Treatment	Vaccination Available?	Other Ways STI is Passed on
Diagnosed by laboratory tests. There are antibiotics that will cure chlamydia. Penicillin does not cure chlamydia.	N/A	Mother-to-child: Chlamydia may pass an eye infection or pneumonia to a baby during a vaginal delivery. To avoid this, mothers can be tested and treated for chlamydia during pregnancy.
Diagnosed by laboratory tests Gonorrhoea can be cured with antibiotics. But recently it has become resistant to several types of antibiotics.	N/A	Mother-to-child: Gonorrhoea may pass an eye infection to a baby during a vaginal birth. The infant's eyes can be treated with silver nitrate at birth to prevent infection.
Diagnosed with a blood test. There are no drugs to treat hepatitis B. It can go away on its own. Or it can remain in the body. Vaccination before infection can prevent getting hepatitis B.	Yes	'Dirty' needles, that is needles that are not sterilised to kill the virus. This can include needles used for: ▪ Taking illegal drugs. ▪ Body piercings. ▪ Tattoos. ▪ Sharing razors or toothbrushes. Mother-to-child: During vaginal birth. The best option is a Caesarean section (C-section) surgical delivery.

STI Name	Type of STI			Description
	Virus	Bacteria	Parasite	
Herpes	X			There are two different types of herpes: HSV1 and HSV2 for short. HSV1 commonly causes cold sores around the lips and mouth. But either HSV1 or HSV2 can cause sores on the genitals. Either type can be passed by any kind of sexual contact. The virus remains in the body for life. Often a person with herpes may have no sores. But the virus can still be passed on to a partner. Possible symptoms: ▨ Tingling in the genital or anal area. ▨ Sores or red or raw areas anywhere on the body. ▨ Small red bumps that become itchy, painful sores and may crust over. ▨ Fever, headache, muscle aches. ▨ Pain or difficulty urinating. ▨ Vaginal discharge. ▨ Swollen glands in the groin. It often causes repeat outbreaks. Symptoms tend to be milder during repeat outbreaks. Herpes is generally not a serious infection. But it can be serious for someone who has HIV.
HIV	X			HIV attacks the white blood cells in the body that fight infection. HIV damages them and makes them unable to defend against diseases. Untreated, HIV can lead to AIDS. Symptoms: ▨ Fever. ▨ Headache. ▨ Tiredness. ▨ Swollen glands in the neck or groin.
HPV	X			HPV is short for human papillomavirus. A papilloma is a wart. There are more than 40 different types of HPV that affect the genitals. They may cause soft, flesh-coloured warts on men's and women's genitals or the anal area. Or they may not. Some cause warts that no one can see. For example, the warts may be inside a woman's vagina. Or they may be on her cervix. Most HPVs are mild. A more serious form of HPV causes warts that can change the cells of the skin's surface. This can cause pre-cancers or cancers. A woman who has this type of HPV has a risk of cancer of the cervix. Though very rare, there is also the possibility of men getting cancers of the penis. There are also rare risks of cancers of the anus, tongue and mouth for both men and women.

Diagnosis and Treatment	Vaccination Available?	Other Ways STI is Passed on
Can be diagnosed by: ▓ A medical exam. ▓ A blood test. ▓ Microscopic exam of sample from a sore. There is no cure for herpes. But there are drugs to treat symptoms. The drugs also can prevent repeat outbreaks. This reduces the chance of passing the virus on.	No	▓ Kissing. ▓ Skin-to-skin. Mother-to-child: A woman who has a recurring genital herpes infection has developed antibodies to the virus. These antibodies will be passed to the foetus through the placenta. The antibodies will protect the baby from herpes infection during a vaginal birth. The danger is if a woman gets her first genital herpes infection late in pregnancy. Then her body will not develop antibodies before the baby's birth. The best option is a C-section delivery. If it is infected with genital herpes during a vaginal birth this can cause serious health problems to a baby. These may include eye, skin, or brain infection and even death.
Diagnosed with a blood test. There are no drugs to cure HIV. But there are several drugs that can reduce the harm the virus does to the immune system. These drugs can significantly reduce the risk of HIV leading to AIDS.	No	'Dirty' needles used for: ▓ Taking illegal drugs. ▓ Body piercings. ▓ Tattoos. Mother-to-child: HIV can be passed on through the placenta, but if the mother takes special drugs during pregnancy this can be prevented. C-section delivery avoids the baby being infected with HIV during a vaginal birth. Bottle feeding is recommended because HIV is also in breast milk.
Diagnosed by: ▓ Medical exam. ▓ Pap smear for women. HPV cannot be treated. The viruses are usually mild. The body is often able to fight them. So, the viruses go away by themselves. For more serious forms of HPV, yearly pap smears identify changes in the cells of the cervix. Pre-cancers and cancers can be easily diagnosed in early stages. They can be removed at that stage.	Yes	Mother-to-child: Rarely HPV may be passed to a baby during a vaginal birth. It can infect the baby's genitals or cause a lung infection.

STI Name	Type of STI			Description
	Virus	Bacteria	Parasite	
Pubic lice			X	Pubic lice are different from head lice. They live mostly in pubic hair. They are tiny, but can be seen with the naked eye. It's more likely to see their droppings. These are black specks.
Syphilis		X		Untreated, syphilis can stay dormant in the human body for many years. During that time, it may cause a person no problems. But the bacteria can still infect any sexual partners. Without treatment, syphilis progresses slowly over many years. It can lead to many different serious diseases including: heart problems, brain infection and dementia – severe memory loss.
Trichomoniasis			X	Trichomoniasis is a one-cell creature that can only be seen under a microscope. It can invade a woman's vagina or a man or woman's urethra. It causes infection where it settles.

Diagnosis and Treatment	Vaccination Available?	Other Ways STI is Passed on
Diagnosed by medical exam. The lice are treated with solutions bought at the chemist's.	N/A	Sharing towels or clothing.
Diagnosed by: ▓ A blood test. ▓ Microscopic exam of sample from a sore. In the early stage, syphilis is easy to cure with penicillin or other antibiotics.	N/A	Mother-to-child: Passed during pregnancy, syphilis can cause miscarriages, premature births or stillbirths. It can also cause death of newborn babies. Some infants born with syphilis have symptoms or deformities at birth. For most, symptoms only show later. Untreated, a child may have many serious health problems.
Diagnosed by: ▓ Laboratory tests. ▓ Medical exam. A single dose of a certain antibiotic cures the infection.	N/A	Mother-to-child: Passed during pregnancy, the bacteria may cause premature births. May be responsible for low-weight births.

Help List

BeingGirl

www.beinggirl.co.uk
A website for girls with straight talk about the body and life changes of puberty.

Brook for Young People

www.brook.org.uk
Email: admin@brook.org.uk
National administration office (not a clinic): 421 Highgate Studios, 53-79 Highgate Road, London NW5 1TL
Helpline: 0808 802 1234 (Monday to Friday, 9am-5pm). Free from all phones, including mobiles. Can also be contacted by Skype.
Brook provides sexual health advice and services to people under 25. Services are free. Your privacy is assured. Brook runs help and information phone lines and a website. The website includes easy-to-understand information about all aspects of sexuality. Clinic services are offered at multiple centres. These are located throughout England, in Jersey and in Northern Ireland. For a centre near you, check the website. Interpreters are available for non-English speakers.

Family Planning Association

www.fpa.org.uk
Online answers to questions about sexual matters.
UK Office
50 Featherstone Street, London EC1Y 8QU
Northern Ireland Offices
3rd Floor, Ascot House, 24–31 Shaftesbury Square, Belfast BT2 7DB
2nd Floor, 67 Carlisle Road, Derry BT48 6JL
Scotland Office
Unit 10, Firhill Business Centre, 76 Firhill Road, Glasgow G20 7BA

Wales Office
Suite D1, Canton House, 435-451 Cowbridge Road East, Cardiff CF5 1JH
Helplines:
England: sexual health direct: 0845 122 8690 (Monday to Friday, 9am to 6pm)
Northern Ireland: 0845 122 8687 (Monday to Friday, 9am to 5pm)

NHS Choices

www.nhs.uk
NHS Choices is a user-friendly online health website. It provides easy-to-understand information on all health topics for all ages.

NHS Direct

www.nhsdirect.nhs.uk
24-hour helpline: 0845 46 47. Call charges apply.
Provides easy-to-understand medical advice for all ages.

Book List

Scientific Advances on Contraceptives for Men
By Pam Belluck. New York Times, 23 July 2011.
Recent news about research on new forms of contraception for men.

Over-the-Counter Vaginal Contraceptive and Spermicide Drug Products Containing Nonoxynol-9; Required Labeling. Final Rule.
United States Food and Drug Administration. Federal Register, 19 Dec. 2007.
Background information on how nonoxynol-9 may increase the risk of HIV infection.

Panel Recommends HPV Vaccine for Boys and Young Men
By Gardiner Harris. New York Times, 25 October 2011.
Recent news about the HPV vaccination.

Guide to Getting it On
By Paul Joannides. Goofy Foot Press, Oregon, USA, Sixth Edition, 2012.
A 900-page book on everything you ever wanted to know about sex. Focused mainly on teens. Written in a straight-forward, easy-to-read style.

The Pill: An Essential Guide
By Jo Johnson. Need2Know, Peterborough, 2008.
A complete guide to all types of contraception pills. Also includes an overview of other contraception methods.

Buzz Kill: How does Alcohol Affect the Teenage Brain?
By Amy Paturel. Neurology Now. Dec. 2011/Jan. 2012. pages 23–28.
A scientific look at the teen brain and how alcohol affects it.

This Beautiful Life
By Helen Shulman. Harper Collins, New York, 2011.
A novel about cybersex gone viral.

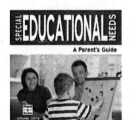
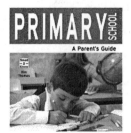

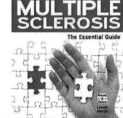